sewNEWS

the trusted sewing source

MAKING A HOUSE a home is all about the accessories and personal touches that are made much simpler with a sewing machine. Fabrics are sure to coordinate, quality is never sacrificed and the end result is much more indicative of you and your style.

In the pages that follow, you'll find over 18 projects to add creativity and ingenuity to every room in your house. From duvet covers to table runners to window treatments and more, you'll find all the instructions you need to fill your home with all the trimmings that make it unique and special to you.

Enjoy and have fun!

For more information, visit **sewnews.com.**

sewNEWS

741 Corporate Circle, Ste. A
Golden, CO, 80401
sewnews.com

SEW NEWS STAFF
Editorial
Editor-in-Chief: Ellen March
Senior Editor: Beth Bradley
Associate Editor: Nicole LaFoille
Web Editor: Jill Case
Editorial Assistant: Jessica Giardino

Art
Creative Director: Sue Dothage
Graphic Designer: Erin Hershey
Assistant Graphic Designer: Courtney Kraig
Illustrator: Melinda Bylow
Photography: Brent Ward, Jessica Grenier, Mellisa Karlin Mahoney
Hair & Makeup Stylist: Angela Lewis

CREATIVE CRAFTS GROUP
Group Publisher &
Community Leader: Kristi Loeffelholz
VP of Content: Helen Gregory
Publisher: June Dudley

OPERATIONS
New Business Manager: Adriana Maldonado
Newsstand Consultant: TJ Montilli
Online Marketing Manager: Jodi Lee
Retail Sales: LaRita Godfrey: (800) 815-3538

F+W MEDIA INC.
Chairman & CEO: David Nussbaum
CFO & COO: James Ogle
President: Sara Domville
President: David Blansfield
Chief Digital Officer: Chad Phelps
VP/E-Commerce: Lucas Hilbert
Senior VP/Operations: Phil Graham
VP/Communications: Stacie Berger

LEISURE ARTS STAFF
Editorial Staff
Vice President of Editorial: Susan White Sullivan
Creative Art Director: Katherine Laughlin
Publications Director: Leah Lampirez
Special Projects Director: Susan Frantz Wiles
Prepress Technician: Stephanie Johnson

Business Staff
President and Chief Executive Officer:
Rick Barton
Senior Vice President of Operations:
Jim Dittrich
Vice President of Finance: Fred F. Pruss
Vice President of Sales-Retail Books:
Martha Adams
Vice President of Mass Market:
Bob Bewighouse
Vice President of Technology and Planning:
Laticia Mull Dittrich
Controller: Tiffany P. Childers
Information Technology Director: Brian Roden
Director of E-Commerce: Mark Hawkins
Manager of E-Commerce: Robert Young
Retail Customer Service Manager: Stan Raynor

Library of Congress Control Number: 2014937333
ISBN-13/EAN: 978-1-4647-1589-1
UPC: 0-28906-06346-2

contents

19

8

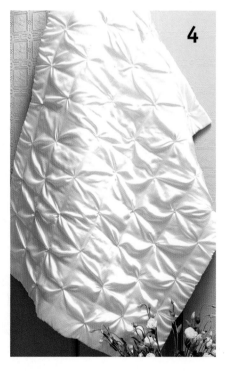

4

44

THE Luxe LIFE

{ by Sandra Geiger }

Give your décor a luxe makeover with a tufted satin throw. Use standard batting or recycle an existing comforter.

Supplies

Supplies listed are enough to make one 48" x72" throw.

- **2 flat queen-size satin sheets or 7 yards of 45"-wide satin fabric**

- **2 yards of 48"-wide high-loft quilt batting (see "Sources.") or a full-size new or recycled comforter**

- **Thread: matching all-purpose and hand quilting**

- **Silk pins**

- **Needles: hand sewing, curved upholstery and beading**

- **Tailor's chalk or removable fabric marker**

- **230 size 4mm pearl or seed beads (optional)**

- **Eighty 8mm hot-fix crystals (optional)**

- **Hot-fix beading tool (optional; see "Sources.")**

Prepare

Use ¹/₂" seam allowances unless otherwise noted.

If using sheets, remove any creases by placing the sheets in a dryer with a damp towel at a low heat setting for 15 minutes, or press using an iron on a low setting.

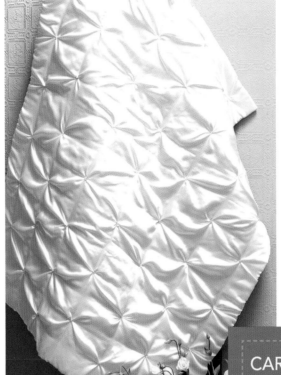

If using fabric, cut two rectangles 63"x the fabric width. Trim off the selvages. With right sides together, stitch one long edge to create a front rectangle that measures 63"x88". Repeat to create one 63"x88" backing rectangle.

Fold the front in half lengthwise with right sides together; press lightly to crease. Fold the fabric in half widthwise with right sides together; press lightly to crease. Unfold.

Position the front right side up on a large flat surface. Draw a line along the lengthwise crease. Draw three lines at a 7" interval to the left of the center line. Repeat to draw three lines to the right of the center line.

Draw a line along the widthwise crease.

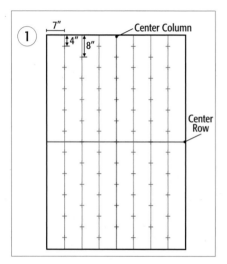

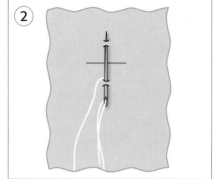

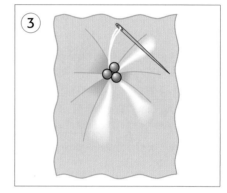

Mark a 1″ crosshatch on the first lengthwise line, 4″ from the upper edge. Continue marking the entire line at a 4″ interval. Mark a crosshatch on the second line 8″ from the upper edge. Continue marking the entire line at 4″ intervals. Repeat to mark the remaining lines, alternating the first crosshatch 4″ and 8″ from the upper edge (1).

Thread the hand sewing needle with quilting thread and knot the end. Bring the needle through the center crosshatch lowest point, center and upper end (2). Pull the thread taut to form a tuck. Tie a small knot. If adding beads, pick up one bead with the needle tip and slide it down to the fabric surface. Secure the bead with several stitches.

Take a stitch at one crosshatch left end, and then stitch another bead at the cross hatch center. Repeat to tuck the remaining crosshatch end and stitch a third bead at the crosshatch center (3).

Repeat to tuck and stitch three beads at each crosshatch, working from the center outward.

Spread out the batting on a large flat surface. Square the front and batting edges if necessary. Pin-mark each batting- and throw-top edge center.

To gather the top to fit the batting, refer to "Great Gathers" at right or baste each top edge, leaving long thread tails. Gently pull the thread tails, evenly distributing the fullness until the top is ½″ larger than the batting along all edges.

Position the backing right side up over the batting, matching the center marks. Square and trim the backing edges so they're ½″ larger than the batting on all edges. Mark each batting edge center.

Position the top right side down over the backing, matching the center marks; pin the perimeter.

Stitch the perimeter through all layers, using a ⅝″ seam allowance to catch the batting outer ½″. This prevents the batting edges from pulling away or rolling. Leave a 14″ opening along one short edge for turning.

Clip the corners and turn the throw right side out. Slipstitch the opening closed.

Place the throw with the backing side facing up on a large surface. Thread the curved needle with quilting thread.

Beginning at the center tuft, take a small stitch through all layers. Knot the thread on the backing side. Repeat to take a stitch at each remaining tuft, working outward from the center.

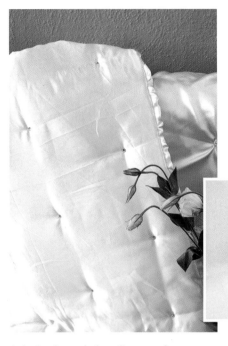

Tip: Omit the beads and crystals if the throw will be used by small children. Instead, stitch the tufts using Perle cotton or metallic thread.

If desired, apply hot-fix crystals over the thread knots, following the manufacturer's instructions.

Comforter Fill

Position the backing wrong side up on a large surface. Position the comforter right side up over the backing. Position the top right side up over the comforter; pin through all layers.

Determine where the comforter stitching lines intersect. Mark the intersections on the front with a crosshatch.

Thread the curved needle with quilting thread. Stitch tufts through all layers at each crosshatch as per the Batting Fill instructions. If desired, add beads to the tufts.

Trim the top and backing edges so they're 1″ larger than the comforter on all edges. Fold the top and backing edges ½″ toward the wrong side; pin.

Thread the hand sewing needle with quilting thread. Abut the folded edges, and then slipstitch to enclose the comforter. ✂

SOURCES
Creative Crystal carries hot-fix crystal applicators: (800) 578-0716, creativecrystal.com.
Fairfield carries bonded polyester batting: (800) 980-8000, poly-fil.com.

GREAT GATHERS

- **Use a couching foot** and cording to create stable, even gathers.

- **Thread the cording** through the couching foot center hole. Thread the needle and bobbin with all-purpose thread.

- **Position the free cording** ½″ from the fabric edge. Set the machine to a 2.5mm- to 3.5mm-wide zigzag stitch.

- **Couch the cording** onto the fabric, leaving 6″ cording tails at the stitching beginning and end.

- **Gently pull the cording tails** to gather the fabric to the required measurement. Knot the tails.

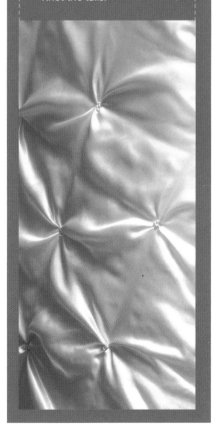

caBIN FEVER

{ by Katrina Walker }

The classic log cabin quilting design enters the modern age when paired with shimmering silk doupioni. Learn a simple single-layer flat-fell seam construction technique to quickly create this bold and beautiful table runner.

About the Design

The log cabin quilting design is a historically significant pattern, with roots reaching back as far as the ancient Egyptians. The design features a central square, sometimes called the "hearth" square, that represents the heart of the home. Traditionally, the hearth square is red. The log cabin variation used in the featured table runner is called "Courthouse Steps" and features bold triangles of color arranged in a diamond design. This radiant pattern is perfect for bringing the dramatic beauty of the fall color palette into your home.

Working with Silk Doupioni

Silk doupioni and its close cousin, shantung, are made from double silk cocoons created by two silkworms spinning next to each another. The double cocoons produce fibers that are more tangled and rough in texture than standard silk, giving doupioni and shantung a distinctive slubbed surface in the crosswise grain.

When sewing silk fabrics, always use sharp, fine tools. Silk quickly dulls cutting blades, so use sharp serrated shears and/or new rotary blades. Use very fine silk pins that have clean, sharp points. Begin each project with a new machine needle, and then change it immediately if it begins to pull threads or labor through the fabric, making a dull punching sound.

Use smooth high-quality thread, such as silk or mercerized cotton, when sewing silk doupioni. High-quality polyester thread works well for most silk projects, but avoid using it to sew seams that will experience stress or stretching during use.

Silk doupioni is hand washable (see "In the Wash" at right), but most doupioni fabrics lose crispness after washing. Dry clean doupioni to maintain the crisp hand, if desired. High-quality doupioni has a tighter, finer weave that withstands washing better than lower quality silk.

Doupioni and shantung fray extensively in the crosswise grain, so carefully handle the fabric to minimize raveling. Because doupioni is prone to fraying and seam slippage, select an appropriate seam construction method. A ¼" seam allowance typically used in quilting is too narrow for doupioni. Instead, use a reinforced or enclosed seam, such as a flat-fell seam, to guard against fraying. Read on to learn an easy flat-fell shortcut that doesn't require trimming or specialty presser feet.

IN THE WASH

Take note of these washing instructions to maintain the silk's lustrous look.

- **Silk is a protein fiber,** similar to hair. For best results, hand wash silk fabric in lukewarm water using a mild soap—not detergent—such as Orvis, Soak, Eucalan or a mild shampoo. Wash each color separately, as excess dye may bleed from the fabric.

- **Rinse well in lukewarm water,** and then roll the fabric in an old towel to remove excess moisture.

- **Hang or lay flat to dry.** Or for a crisper finish, use an iron to press the damp silk dry.

Tip: Cut a ½"-wide strip from a recycled file folder to use as a pressing template.

Table Runner

Supplies
Supplies listed are enough to make one 12"x36" runner.

- Fat quarter of silk doupioni (A)
- 2 fat quarters of coordinating silk doupioni for the widthwise strips (B)
- 2 fat quarters of coordinating silk doupioni for the lengthwise strips (C)
- Coordinating decorative polyester thread
- Size 80/12 Microtex needle (If using metallic thread, use an 80/12 metallic needle.)
- Edgestitch foot (optional)

Cut
From fabric A, cut three 4½" squares. Cut fabric B and fabric C fat quarters into 3"-wide strips.

Construct
Fold one fabric A square edge ½" toward the wrong side. Repeat to press the opposite edge ½" toward the wrong side **(1)**.

Insert one fabric B strip into one fold with right sides together. Stitch ½" from the fold through all layers **(2)**. Don't worry if the square raw edge

isn't entirely caught in the stitching, as it's more important to maintain the consistent ½" distance from the fold. Press to set the stitches.

Fold the fabric B strip toward the right side, concealing the raw edges; press **(3)**.

Edgestitch the first fabric A fold on the fabric right side **(4)**. There are now two stitching lines on the fabric right side, and one stitching line on the wrong side.

Repeat to attach a fabric B strip to the remaining fabric A folded edge to complete the first center panel. Trim the fabric B strips even with the fabric A square edges **(5)**.

Fold one panel long edge ½" toward the wrong side; press. **Note:** The panel right side features the double stitching lines.

Insert one fabric C strip into the panel fold with right sides together **(6)**. Stitch ½" from folded edge; press to set the stitches.

Fold the fabric C strip toward the right side, concealing the raw edges; press. Edgestitch the first panel fold on the fabric right side.

Repeat to attach a second fabric C strip to the remaining panel long edge. Trim the fabric C strips even with the panel edges.

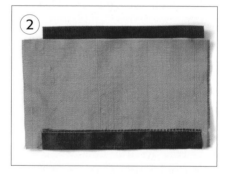

Continue piecing the block, using the flat-fell seam technique to attach two more pairs each of fabric B and fabric C strips **(7).**

Repeat to piece two additional blocks. Designate one block as the center block. Fold the center block pieced edges (containing both fabric B and C) $\frac{1}{2}''$ toward the wrong side; press.

Position one side block pieced edge into one center-block fold with right sides together, matching the seamlines. Stitch $\frac{1}{2}''$ from the folded edge; press to set the stitches.

Fold the side block toward the right side, concealing the raw edges; press. Edgestitch along the center-block first fold.

Repeat to attach the remaining side block. If necessary, evenly trim the runner edges.

Finish

To finish the runner perimeter, stitch a $\frac{5}{16}''$-wide double-folded hem or bind the raw edges using the remaining fabric. ✄

Tip: To change the runner size, vary the central square or strip sizes, or add more pieced blocks.

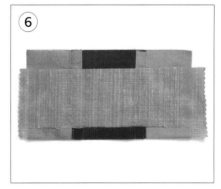

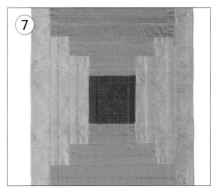

Beauty & BATIK

(by Shannon Dennis)

Decorate your table with organic colors of batik fabric, delicate 3-D leaves and reverse-appliqué leaf details.

Tip: Use different batik colors to make the leaf embellishments pop.

Supplies

- **2 yards each of coordinating batiks (A & B)**
- **⅓ yard each of 5 coordinating batiks**
- **All-purpose cotton thread**
- **Double-sided fusible web**
- **Removable fabric marker**
- **Tube turner (optional; see "Sources.")**
- **Seam sealant (optional)**

Cut

From fabrics A and B, cut two 12″ x 18″ rectangles each for the sides and one 18″ x 20″ rectangle each for the center.

From each of the coordinating batiks, cut one strip measuring 1½″ x the fabric width, one strip measuring 2½″ x the fabric width and one strip measuring 4″ x the fabric width.

Construct

Use ½″ seam allowances unless otherwise noted.

Fold one coordinating batik strip in half lengthwise with right sides together; pin, and then stitch the long edge using a ⅛″ seam allowance. Using a tube turner (or referring to "Tube Turning" at right), turn the tube to the right side. Repeat to stitch the remaining coordinating batik strips. Center each seam; press. Cut each tube into 11″-long strips.

Position one fabric A small rectangle right side up on a flat work surface. Abut one strip end to one rectangle long edge ½″ from the rectangle short edge. Continue to pin strips to the rectangle, alternating sizes and colors as desired, and leaving at least ¼″ to ½″ of space between each strip. Baste the abutted strip ends to the rectangle, leaving the opposite ends free. Repeat to add strips to the remaining fabric A small rectangle.

With right sides together, align one fabric B small rectangle with one fabric A small rectangle, sandwiching the strips; pin. Stitch the perimeter, catching the basted strip ends in the stitching. Leave a 4″ opening along one short edge for turning **(1)**. Clip the corners and turn the side panel right side out through the opening; press. Fold the opening raw edges ½″ toward the wrong side; press. Topstitch ⅛″ from the perimeter, closing the opening with the stitches. Repeat to stitch the remaining side panel.

Position fabric A large rectangle on a flat work surface with the right side facing up. Position one side panel over the rectangle with the right

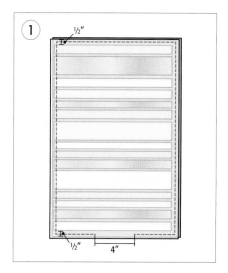

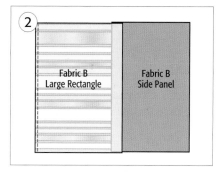

side facing up and the side-panel free strip ends matching the left rectangle long edge. Position the fabric B large rectangle right side over the side panel, matching the fabric A rectangle edges. Pin the sandwich generously. Stitch the rectangle left edge through all layers **(2)**.

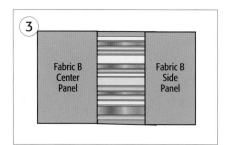

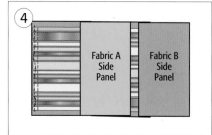

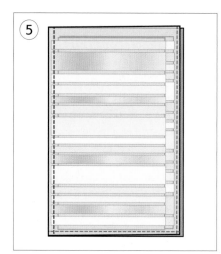

Unfold the fabric B rectangle long raw edge to the right side (3). Position the remaining side panel over the fabric B rectangle, matching the strip ends with the rectangle long raw edge; pin and then baste (4).

Stuff the side panels between the center-panel layers. With right sides together, stitch the center panels along the basted edge and the upper short edge (5).

Turn the table runner to the right side through the center-panel lower open edge; press. Fold the opening raw edges $1/2''$ toward the wrong side; press. Top-stitch $1/8''$ from the perimeter, closing the opening with the stitches.

Reverse Appliqué Leaf

Copy the leaf templates on page 15.

Using a removable fabric marker, position one leaf template on the table runner right side; trace. Pin together the fabric A and fabric B layers around the leaf outline.

Select a 2.5mm straight stitch on the machine. Stitch over the outline.

Using a pair of appliqué scissors, carefully trim away the upper fabric layer close to the stitches, being careful not to cut through the lower fabric. Apply a thin layer of seam sealant to the raw edges, if desired.

3-D Leaf

Use the leaf templates on page 15.

Using batik fabric scraps, cut several 5" squares and 7" squares for the small and large leaf embellishments, respectively. Each leaf requires two squares.

Fuse two squares with wrong sides together using fusible web, following the manufacturer's instructions. Position one small leaf template over one small square; trace the template, and then cut out. Repeat to create as many leaves as desired. The featured table runner showcases four small leaves and five large leaves.

Stitch each leaf center along the table runner as desired. ✄

TUBE TURNING

Learn creative ways to turn narrow tubes without using a store-bought tube turner.

Safety Pin
Attach a safety pin to one tube end. Push the pin through the tube, rolling the fabric over itself; press. A safety pin works best with tightly woven fabrics, such as cotton, wool and silk.

Serger Stitch
Serge a chain of stitches a few inches longer than the tube. While the thread chain is attached to the serger, move it to the front of the serger and place it inside the fabric. Fold the tube in half and serge the long edge. Turn the tube right side out by gently pulling the serged chain. This technique works well with knits and very narrow tubes, such as spaghetti straps.

Chopstick
Turn the tube end $1/2''$ toward the right side. Using a chopstick, gently push the unturned tube through the opening.

Hemostat
This medical tool works well for turning very narrow tubes. Pinch one tube end, and then guide the hemostat through the tube, pushing the fabric over itself.

SOURCES

Fasturn, LLC. provided the tube turner: (800) 729-0280, fasturn.net.

Hoffman Fabrics provided batik fabric: (800) 547-0100, hoffmanfabrics.com.

Leaf Templates

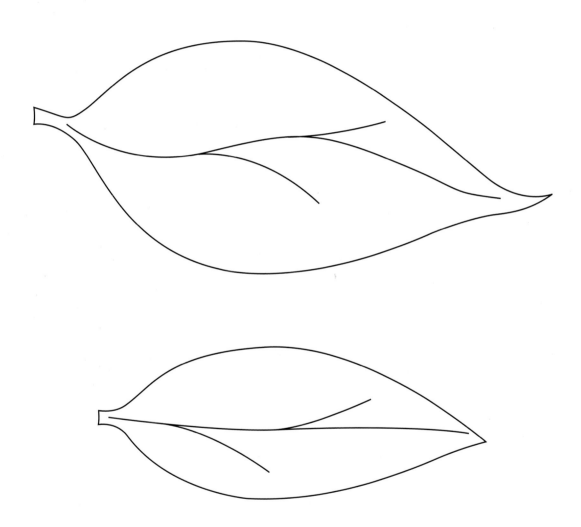

WELL
rounded

{ by Pam Damour }

A scalloped edge adds
an elegant touch to a basic
tablecloth. Learn simple techniques for
placing and stitching perfect scallops.

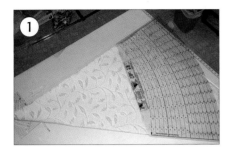

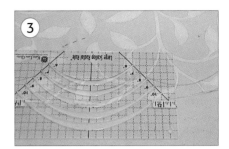

Supplies

Supplies listed are enough to make one 90"-diameter tablecloth.

- 5½ yards of solid or 6 yards of print 54"-wide home-décor fabric
- 5¼ yard of coordinating 54"-wide home-décor lining fabric
- Large radial ruler (See "Sources.") or a plate at least 9" in diameter
- Matching polyester thread
- Pencil or removable fabric marker
- Circular tablecloth template (optional; see "Sources.")

Cut

If using solid fabric, cut two rectangles measuring 90"x the fabric width. If using a print fabric, see "Match Maker" on page 18 for cutting and print-matching directions.

Cut one rectangle in half lengthwise. With right sides together, stitch one small rectangle to one large rectangle long edge. Repeat to attach the remaining small rectangle to the large rectangle opposite long edge. Press open the seams.

Repeat to cut and piece the lining fabric, leaving a 10" opening along one seam for turning.

With right sides together, fold the pieced rectangle in half and then in fourths. Fold the rectangle in half on

the diagonal to form a triangle. Use the circular template to draw the curve for a 91"-diameter circle, following the manufacturer's instructions (1). If not using a circular template, mark the triangle folded edge 45½" from the center. Continue to mark several points 45½" from the center, and then connect the marks to form the curved cutting line.

Repeat to fold and draw the curve on the lining rectangle. Cut out the fabric and lining circles.

Construct

Align the fabric and lining circles with right sides together; pin. Fold the circles in half with the fabric side facing out, and then fold in half again.

If using a plate to draw the scallops, turn the plate upside down. Use masking tape to mark the plate at 7" in diameter (2).

To draw the first scallop, position the radial ruler or upside-down plate at one folded corner, aligning the 7" slot or plate curve lowest point approximately 1" from the raw edge. Draw the scallop curve by tracing the template slot or the plate edge between the tape marks.

Reposition the template or plate to draw a second consecutive scallop (3). Repeat to draw a total of ten 7"-wide scallops along the circle edge. Refold the circle to draw ten scallops on each remaining fourth.

FACING FIX

If you're unable to find lining fabric that closely matches the tablecloth fabric color, add a facing to camouflage the contrasting outer edges.

- **From the home-décor fabric,** cut enough 4"-wide bias strips to equal the circle circumference. With right sides together, piece the strips along the short edges.
- **Fold one strip long edge** ½" toward the wrong side; press.
- **Before sandwiching** the fabric and lining circles with right sides together, position the strip wrong side down around the lining circle right-side perimeter, aligning the raw edges; pin. Stitch close to the strip folded edge through both layers.
- **Continue constructing** the tablecloth as directed.

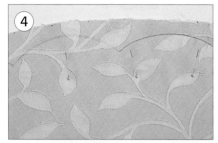

Unfold the circle. Stitch along the scallop marks through both layers **(4)**.

Trim the circle a scant ¼" beyond the stitching line. Clip a small "V" at each scallop intersection **(5)**.

Finish

Turn the tablecloth right side out through the lining opening; press. Hand stitch the opening closed. ✀

SOURCES

Katie Lane Quilts carries Scallop Radial Rules: (603) 673-2867, katielane.com.

Pam Damour carries the Circular Tablecloth Template: (518) 297-2699, pamdamour.com.

MATCH MAKER

When using a print fabric, extra yardage is needed in order to match the pattern at the seams. Follow these steps to perfectly align the print for a virtually invisible seam.

- **Determine the width** of the vertical print repeat (the distance between the beginning and end of one complete pattern in the print or design). The featured fabric has a 14½"-wide vertical repeat.

- **Cut each fabric rectangle** to the length of the next full vertical repeat beyond 90". For a 14½"-wide repeat, 6 repeats equals 87", so it's necessary to cut 7 full repeats to equal 101½". Cut one rectangle in half lengthwise.

- **Determine where the print** repeat begins along one large rectangle selvage edge. At this point, fold the long edge toward the wrong side; press.

- **Position one small rectangle** selvage edge under the large rectangle folded edge, carefully aligning the print on the fabric right side; pin close to the fold **(A)**.

- **Position the large rectangle** over the small rectangle with right sides together, sandwiching the pins. Pin or baste the selvage edges close to the foldline.

- **Stitch directly over the large rectangle** foldline, carefully removing the first row of pins between the fabric layers as you stitch **(B)**.

- **Inspect the pattern alignment** on the fabric right side **(C)**. Press open the seam and trim off the selvages. Repeat to attach the remaining small rectangle.

- **Continue constructing** the tablecloth as directed.

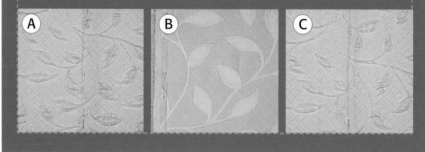

CURVY COORDINATES

Use the scallop technique to create unique edges on other home-dec items. Vary the depth and size of the scallops according to the project size and desired look.

- **Add an elegant touch** to bedroom décor by stitching a scalloped border on a pillow sham. For a regal framed effect, stitch a pleated ruffle around the inner sham perimeter.

- **Make a simple matching** neck roll pillow extra special by adding scalloped edges finished with piping. Set off the scallops by embellishing the pillow ends with complementary braid trim.

UNDER
cover

{ by Carol Zentgraf }

Create custom slipcovers to
update a worn-out chair or
dress up your dining room
for spring.

Supplies

- Chair (without arms)
- 54"-wide home-décor fabric (amount according to measurements)
- 3/16"-diameter piping (amount according to measurements)
- All-purpose thread
- Pattern tracing cloth
- Removable fabric marker

Measure

Measure the chair front and sides to determine the slipcover panel measurements (1):

- Inner back (A): Measure the inner chair-back width including the side edges; add 4″ to determine the inside-back panel width. *Note:* If the chair back is angled, measure the widest and narrowest parts and cut the panel at an angle to fit. Measure the inner chair-back length from the upper edge to the seat lower edge; add 6″ to determine the inner-back panel length. Record the inner-back panel measurements.

- Outer back (B): Measure the outer chair-back width; add 4″ to determine the back panel width. *Note:* If the chair back is angled, measure the widest and narrowest parts and cut the panel at an angle to fit. Measure the outer chair-back length from the upper edge to the seat lower edge; add 6″ to determine the outer-back panel length. Record the outer-back panel measurements.

- Seat (C): Measure the seat width and depth including the side edges; add 4″ to determine the seat panel width. *Note:* If the chair seat is angled, measure the widest and narrowest parts and cut the panel at an angle to fit. Measure the seat length and front depth; add 6″ to determine the seat

panel length. Record the seat panel measurements.

- Skirt (D): Measure the chair seat lower-edge width along each side; add 12″ to determine the skirt-panel width. Measure the length from the chair seat lower edge to the floor; add 2½″ to determine the skirt-panel length. You'll need four skirt panels.

Cut

Using the recorded measurements, draw the panels on pattern tracing cloth; label. Cut out the panel patterns.

Measure the panels to determine the amount of yardage needed; allow additional yardage for centering prints, if desired. Add an additional ½ yard for bias strips to create the piping. To determine the piping yardage, measure the outer-back panel perimeter and the seat-panel side and front edges.

Cut the inner-back, outer-back and seat panels from the fabric, placing any print motifs as desired. Cut four skirt panels, making sure that the print will flow continuously when the short edges are pieced together, if applicable. Label each panel wrong side.

Cut enough 1³/₈"-wide bias strips to equal the determined piping yardage including ½″ seam allowances when pieced. Piece the strips along the short ends with right sides together. Wrap the strip around the piping with wrong sides together; baste close to the piping.

Construct

Use ½″ seam allowances unless otherwise noted.

Position the chair so the outer-back is facing up, using another chair seat for stability if needed. Center the outer-back panel over the chair outer-back; pin the fabric to the chair edges (2).

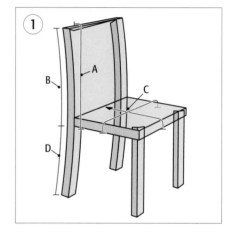

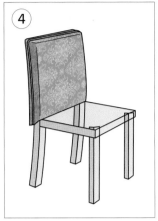

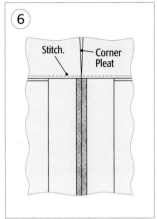

Stitch. | Corner Pleat

Position the chair upright. Center the inner-back panel over the chair inner-back with the panel upper edge extending 4″ above the chair upper edge. Pin the inner- and outer-back panel sides and upper edges together, folding pleats in the inner-back panel upper corners to fit around the chair upper corners (3).

Draw a line on the inner-back panel connecting the pins; mark the pleat placement. Remove the panels from the chair back. True the drawn line, and then trim the fabric ½″ beyond the line.

Unpin the panels. Transfer the pleat markings to the inner-front panel wrong side. Refold the pleats with right sides together, and then stitch. Place the inner-front panel on the chair to check the upper corner fit; adjust if needed. Trim the excess pleat fabric from the wrong side.

Position the inner-front panel right side up. Position piping along the panel sides and upper edge, aligning the raw edges; pin. Baste close to the piping. Place the panel on the chair to make sure the piping aligns with the chair-back edge; adjust if needed (4).

With right sides together, stitch the inner-back and outer-back

panel sides and upper edges. Turn right side out; press.

Place the back cover over the chair back. On the inner-back panel, draw a line along the inner-seat back lower edge, trim the excess fabric 1″ beyond the line. Extend each marked line end diagonally to connect to the seat-back lower corners. On the outer-back panel, draw a line along the outer-back seat lower edge. Remove the cover and trim the fabric ½″ beyond the marked lines

Place the seat panel right side up on the chair seat, centering the print motifs as desired. Pin the seat panel in place along the seat sides and front edge. Draw a line along the seat back, and extend each line end diagonally to connect to the seat-back lower corners (5). Pleat the seat-panel front edges to fit over the seat corners; pin and mark the pleats. Remove the cover; trim the fabric ½″ from the marked lines.

With right sides together, stitch the front corner pleats. With right sides together, stitch the seat panel to the inner-front panel lower edge; press.

Place the cover on the chair. On the seat panel, draw a line along the seat lower edge. Trim the fabric ½″ beyond the line.

Position piping along the seat-panel right side lower edge, aligning the raw edges; pin. Baste close to the piping.

With right sides together, piece the skirt panel short edges. Press open the seams.

Pin-mark each skirt-panel upper-edge center. Pin-mark each cover-panel lower-edge center. With right sides together, pin the skirt to the cover, matching the center marks. Pin from each center mark to each corner. Stitch, leaving the excess fabric at each corner free.

To create a box pleat at each corner, turn the cover to the wrong side. Flatten the excess fabric at each corner, aligning each skirt seam with each corner-pleat seam; pin. Stitch the pleat upper edges along the previous skirt stitching line (6).

Finish

Place the slipcover on the chair to check the length. Trim the lower edge for a 2″ hem allowance. Double-fold the lower edge 1″ toward the wrong side; press. Stitch close to the first fold.

Press the skirt piping seams toward the skirt; topstitch.

PAPER OR
PLASTIC

{ by Carol Zentgraf }

Go green when you make a trio of stylish recycling bins. The easy-to-clean laminated cotton fabric liner is removable for easy emptying.

Tip: Create more bins for other recyclables, such as aluminum and cardboard.

Supplies

Supplies listed are enough to make one 12″x 12″x 20″ recycling bin.

• ⅞ yard of 54″-wide home-décor fabric

• 1 yard of 54″-wide laminated cotton fabric

• Four 12″ x 20″ rectangles & one 12″ square of cardboard

• All-purpose thread

• 3 yards of ½″-wide double-sided fusible web tape

• 2″-wide clear packing tape

Cut

From the home-décor fabric, cut four 13″ x 20½″ rectangles and one 13″ square for the cover.

From the laminated cotton fabric, cut four 13″ x 24″ rectangles and one 13″ square for the liner.

Construct

Use ⅜″ seam allowances unless otherwise noted.

Abut two cardboard rectangle long edges; tape to secure. Repeat to tape the remaining cardboard rectangle long edges to create a box; designate one end as the lower edge. Abut the cardboard square perimeter with the box lower edge; tape to secure.

With right sides together, align two cover rectangle long edges; stitch, beginning ⅜″ from the lower edge. Repeat to stitch the remaining two cover rectangles.

With right sides together, align the cover panels; stitch the free long edges, beginning ⅜″ from the lower edge. Press open the seams.

With right sides together, pin the cover square perimeter to the cover lower edges; stitch, and then press open the seams.

Adhere fusible web tape to the cover wrong-side upper edge, following the manufacturer's instructions. Turn the cover right side out.

Slide the cover over the box, aligning the seams with the box edges and the cover upper edge with the box upper edge. Remove the fusible web paper backing, and then fuse the cover to the box.

With right sides together, align two liner rectangle long edges; stitch ½″ from the raw edges, beginning ½″ from the lower edge. Repeat to stitch the remaining two liner rectangles.

LABEL MAKER

Customize the recycling totes with machine embroidered labels for quick sorting.

Supplies
- Tear-away stabilizer
- Rayon embroidery thread
- Removable fabric marker
- Alphabet embroidery designs: 2"- to 3"-tall letters

EMBROIDER

Before constructing the cover, fold one cover rectangle in half lengthwise and width-wise with right sides together; unfold. Mark the foldlines with a removable fabric marker.

Hoop the rectangle with a piece of stabilizer, centering the foldline inter-section within the hoop. Place the hoop onto the machine.

Spell out "Plastic," "Paper" or "Glass" on the machine screen or in embroidery software. Adjust the lettering height and width as desired; making sure the phrase is less than 11"-long. Save the phrase in the appropriate machine format. Load the alphabet into the machine.

Thread the machine with rayon embroidery thread. Embroider the phrase. Once the embroidery is complete, remove the hoop from the machine and the fabric from the hoop. Carefully tear away the stabilizer beyond the design perimeter.

Finish constructing the cover as instructed below.

With right sides together, align the liner panels; stitch the free long edge, beginning ³⁄₈" from the lower edge. Press open the seams.

With right sides together, pin the liner square perimeter to the liner lower edges; stitch, and then press open the seams.

Adhere fusible web tape to the liner wrong-side upper edge. Fold the upper

TIP: Press laminated cotton on a low-heat setting using a press cloth to avoid melting the vinyl coating.

edge ¹⁄₂" toward the wrong side; press using a press cloth, being careful not to touch the laminated cotton fabric directly with the iron. Remove the fusible web paper backing, and then cover the upper edge with a press cloth; press to fuse the upper edge. Topstitch ³⁄₈" from the fold.

Finish
Place the liner into the box, aligning the seams with the box corners. Fold the liner upper edge 3" over the box upper edge with right sides facing out.

To clean the liner, machine wash in cold water and line dry or tumble

dry on low heat. Or wipe down the laminated cotton with a damp cloth and mild cleanser. Always check with the fabric manufacturer for specific cleaning instructions. ✄

DESIGN
Lettering: Embroidery Arts, Romanesque 6 Design Pack AL711A-Z; embroidery.com

SOURCES
Sulky of America provided the rayon embroidery thread and Tear-Easy stabilizer: (800) 874-4115, sulky.com.
The Warm Company provided Steam-A-Seam 2 double-sided fusible web and double-sided fusible web tape and Steam-A-Seam fusible web: (425) 248-2424, warmcompany.com.
Westminster Fibers provided the Ty Pennington Impressions collection home-dec and laminated cotton fabrics: westminsterfibers.com.

LOVELY LAMPSHADE

{ by Lynne Farris }

Update and refresh a room's décor with a lampshade makeover. Save money by using fabric from your stash while customizing the lampshade to coordinate with the room.

Get Started

Use a plain paper or fabric covered shade and remove any trim or embellishments before measuring. When the lamp is on, imperfections may show through, so finish all edges and trim excess fabric.

Select woven fabrics, such as muslin, linen or cotton. Avoid slinky knits because they will stretch or sag over time.

Use permanent fabric glue, such as Fabri-tac, to ensure a permanent and secure bond. ✂

INSTANT GRATIFICATION

For an instant shade swap, stitch a decorative bead at each corner of a sheer or printed square scarf, and then position the scarf over a small lamp for a dramatic, romantic change.

STRAIGHT SHADE

To create a simple, soft gathered straight drum shade, measure the shade height and circumference; record. Cut a fabric rectangle that measures the height plus 1H"x1H"x the circumference.

With right sides together, stitch the rectangle short ends to form a tube, and then sew gathering stitches along the tube upper and lower edges.

Slip the tube over the shade and draw up the gathering stitches to fit. Secure the cover with clothespins **(1)**.

Glue the gathered edges along the shade upper and lower edges; let the glue dry completely.

Trim any excess fabric from the shade edges. Conceal the upper and lower edges by gluing a coordinating ribbon, such as grosgrain, a strip of bias tape or a decorative trim over the raw edges.

TAPERED SHADE

To create a pattern, position the shade on a large piece of plain paper so that the shade seam is at the lower left corner.

Mark the upper and lower shade edges, and then slowly roll the shade while continuing to mark the arc.

Add ¾" to the curved edges and ½" to one straight edge **(2)**.

Cut out the pattern and position it on the fabric wrong side, aligning one pattern straight edge with the fabric grain; trace the pattern.

Align the fabric straight edge with the shade seam and glue along the upper and lower edges.

To finish the edges, trim the excess fabric and glue bias tape or decorative trim along the shade upper and lower edges.

SOURCE
Beacon Adhesives provided the Fabri-Tac permanent adhesive: (800) 865-7238, beaconcreates.com.

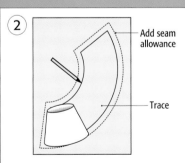

Clothespins

Grosgrain ribbon

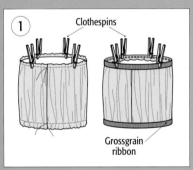

Add seam allowance

Trace

Create a teatime ensemble that's not only functional, but also absolutely adorable. Reinforce the tea theme with cute coordinating fabrics. Use insulated batting to keep tea warm during an afternoon of scones and gossip.

TEAtime

{ by Kate Van Fleet }

Tea Tales

It stands to reason that the tea cozy was invented when teatime was introduced and practiced daily in mid-1800s England. But according to Irish legend, a farmer may have invented the concept as early as 1600. The farmer reached across the table to grab the teapot and his hat fell over it. Consequently, the tea was kept very warm throughout dinner and the tea cozy was born.

Nowadays, tea cozies are typically solely decorative, as many people use teakettles that remain on the stove without transferring the tea to a ceramic pot. But sometimes it's fun to have a tea party with friends, bring out the fine china or coordinating stoneware and decorate with special linens. The featured projects also make a great gift. Add some homemade goodies and specialty teas with matching mugs in a nice basket and give it to a friend for her birthday, May Day or Mother's Day.

Tea Cozy
Supplies

- ½ yard each of fabric & lining
- ½ yard of insulated batting (See "Source.")
- Coordinating all-purpose thread
- 2 decorative buttons
- Hand sewing needle
- ½"-wide matching double-fold bias tape (optional)
- Pattern tracing cloth or butcher paper (optional)

Prepare

Create a pattern to fit a teapot referring to "Measure Up" below.

MEASURE UP

Measure the teapot circumference around the largest part, the top and the bottom; divide by 2, and then add ½" for seam allowances. (The bottom measurement must equal at least half of the base circumference.)

Measure the teapot height and add ½". Using a piece of pattern tracing cloth or butcher paper, draw a rectangle that measures the new teapot height x the largest part width. Draw lines denoting the top and bottom width, centering the lines across the rectangle **(A)**.

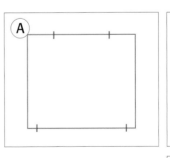

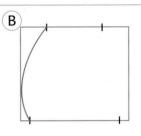

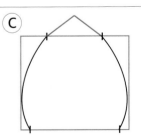

To create the pattern sides, connect the top, largest part and bottom line ends by drawing a curved line along one side edge **(B)**. Fold the pattern in half lengthwise with wrong sides facing. Trace the curved line on the opposite side edge, creating a symmetrical pattern. Unfold the pattern.

Connect the pattern upper edge by drawing angled lines, creating a triangle **(C)**. Cut out the side pattern.

Using another piece of tracing cloth or paper, trace the teapot base and draw a circle 1" beyond the traced line for the seam allowance. Cut out the base pattern.

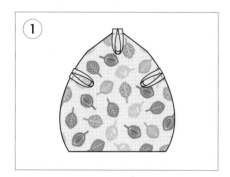

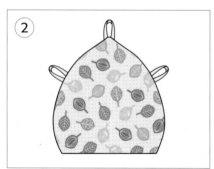

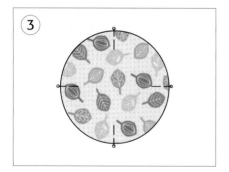

From the fabric, cut four sides, two bases and three 1⅛"x12" strips for the button loops. From the insulated batting, cut two sides and one base.

Construct

Fold each fabric strip in half lengthwise with right sides facing. Stitch the long edge, and then turn right side out. Center the seam along one side; press. Fold each strip in half widthwise, matching the ends.

Measure from the teapot base to the handle upper edge and add 1". Measure and mark this point on one side piece along the right and left edge to denote the button loop placements.

Position one marked side piece on a flat work surface with the marked side facing up. Place a button loop on the side piece at each mark, aligning the raw edges. Place the remaining button loop at the side piece upper point, aligning the raw edges (1). Baste each loop in place. This is the back side.

Position the two remaining side pieces on a flat work surface with right sides together. Place one interfacing side piece over the fabric layers. Stitch the perimeter using a ¼" seam allowance and leaving the lower edge

free. Clip the corners and curves, and then turn right side out, sandwiching the interfacing between the fabric layers; press (2).

Repeat to stitch the back-side piece to the remaining fabric and interfacing side pieces, sandwiching the button loops in the stitching. Clip the corners and curves, and then turn right side out; press.

Sandwich the interfacing base between the fabric base wrong sides. Stitch the perimeter using a ⅛" seam allowance and leaving a 2" opening for turning. Clip the opening seam allowance. Turn the base right side out through the opening, and then fold the opening seam allowances toward the wrong side; press.

Fold the base in quarters and pin-mark each quarter mark along the outer edge (3). Position one side piece lower edge along the base, matching two adjacent pins with the seams; pin. Repeat to pin the remaining side piece lower edge to the base opposite edge.

Hand stitch the base to the sides using a slipstitch or whipstitch. If desired, and for more reinforcement and stability, bind the sewn edge using bias tape.

With the wrong side facing out, hand stitch the front and back pieces together for 1″, beginning at the lower edge **(4)**. Turn the cozy right side out.

Place the teapot into the cozy and wrap the sides around the teapot. Wrap the button loops around to the plain side and mark the button placements. Hand stitch the buttons in place.

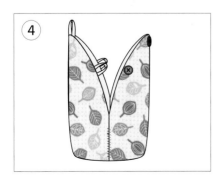

Tablecloth

Supplies

- 1¼ yard of print cotton fabric
- Matching all-purpose thread

Construct

Double-fold each fabric edge ¼″ toward the wrong side, mitering the corners. Stitch the tablecloth perimeter close to the first fold. Press the tablecloth.

Napkins

Supplies listed are enough to make four napkins.

Supplies

- 1 yard of print cotton fabric
- Matching all-purpose thread

Construct

From the fabric, cut four 14″ squares. Double-fold each fabric edge ¼″ toward the wrong side, mitering the corners. Stitch each napkin perimeter close to the fold. Press each napkin. ✂

RESOURCES
Koffee Klatsch, "Tea Cozy/Tea Cozies:" koffeeklatsch.com

Learn About Tea, "Tea Cozy—For Your Teapot:" learn-about-tea.com

SOURCE
The Warm Company provided the Insul~Bright insulated batting: (425) 248-2424, warmcompany.com.

PUMPKIN PATCH

{ by Danielle Thompson }

Decorate your home with a fast and fabulous fall pumpkin patch. Combine fabric prints, textures and colors to craft a clever collection.

VERY VINTAGE

Add interest and texture by whipstitching a doily to a pumpkin.

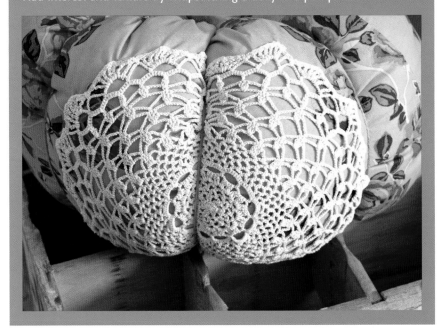

Tip: Use unique fabrics, such as vintage sheets and curtains, burnout velvet or upholstery fabric, for a distinct appearance

Supplies

Supplies listed are enough to make six coordinating pumpkins.

- ½ yard of coordinating print fabric (A)
- ½ yard of solid fabric (B)
- 2 coordinating print fat quarters (C & D)
- 2 coordinating print fat eighths (E & F)
- 12 yards of coordinating yarn
- 6 yards of coordinating embroidery floss
- Polyester fiberfill

Cut

From fabric A, cut one 18″x36″ rectangle for the 36″ pumpkin.

From fabric B, cut one 15″x30″ rectangle for the 30″ pumpkin.

From fabric C, cut one 11″x22″ rectangle for the 22″ pumpkin.

From fabric D, cut one 10″x20″ rectangle for the 20″ pumpkin.

From fabric E, cut one 9″x18″ rectangle for the 18″ pumpkin.

From fabric F, cut one 6″x12″ rectangle for the 12″ pumpkin.

Cut two large stems, two medium stems and two small stems from the remaining fabric scraps, using the templates on page 32.

Construct

Using a long basting stitch, stitch ½″ from the fabric A rectangle long edge, leaving 4″-long thread tails.

Fold the rectangle in half widthwise with right sides together. Stitch the short edges ½″ from the raw edge, and then press.

Using a long basting stitch, stitch ½″ from the lower edge, leaving 4″-long thread tails.

Gently pull the thread tails to gather the lower edge, working from both ends toward the center until the edge is completely gathered. Stitch ⅜″ from the raw edge over the gathering stitches to secure (1).

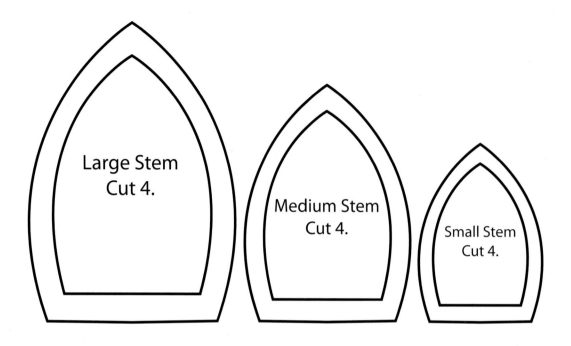

Large Stem
Cut 4.

Medium Stem
Cut 4.

Small Stem
Cut 4.

Turn the pumpkin right side out. Stuff fiberfill into the pumpkin cavity until full.

Gently pull the thread tails to gather the upper edge, working from both ends toward the center until the upper edge is completely closed. Knot the thread ends to secure; trim (2).

Thread the hand embroidery needle with a length of yarn; knot the end. Bring the needle through the pumpkin lower center and pull it through the pumpkin upper center. Bring the needle through the pumpkin lower center again, wrapping the pumpkin with the yarn and pulling tightly to create a defined pumpkin section (3).

Repeat to create seven evenly spaced pumpkin sections. Tie off the yarn at the pumpkin lower center. Evenly distribute the fabric around the yarn sections to create a smooth pumpkin.

With right sides together, stitch ¼" around the large pumpkin stem, leaving

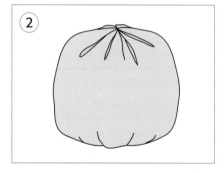

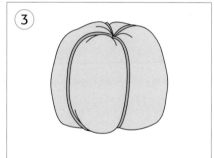

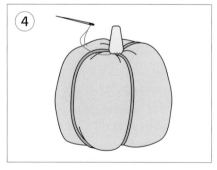

the lower edge open. Clip the seam allowance curve, turn right side out, and then stuff fiberfill into the pumpkin stem until full. Stitch ¼" from the lower-edge opening.

Hand stitch the stem to the pumpkin upper-edge center (4).

Repeat to create the remaining pumpkins. Stitch the large stem on the 30" pumpkin, the medium stems on the 22" and 20" pumpkins and the small stems on the 18" and 12" pumpkins. ✄

Tip: Create any size pumpkin by cutting the fabric rectangle length twice as long as the width.

DECOUPAGE
Letters

{ by Ellen March }

If you have fabric scraps that are too small to incorporate into a project, use them to make fun fabric letters. Spell the words "EAT" for kitchen charm, "SEW" for sewing room inspiration or "LOVE" for bedroom décor.

Supplies

- 12" papier-mâché letter(s) (See "Sources.")
- Fabric scraps in assorted colors & sizes
- Decoupage medium (See "Sources.")
- Foam brush
- Small disposable paint tray
- Disposable tablecloth, newspaper or trash bag
- Brass-plated hangers (optional)

Create

Protect a flat work surface by placing a disposable tablecloth, newspaper or trash bag over it; tape to secure, if desired.

Pour ¼ cup of decoupage medium into a paint tray. Using the foam brush, paint a fabric scrap wrong side with the medium. Position the scrap on the letter. Brush more medium on the fabric right side, making sure to adhere it completely to the letter. Follow the manufacturer's instructions to ensure satisfactory results.

Repeat to add more fabric scraps until the letter is completely covered. Clip into the fabric when covering corners and curves to eliminate any puckers or wrinkles.

Let the letter dry. If desired, paint the entire letter surface with an additional layer of decoupage; let dry.

Repeat to create additional letters to spell out the desired phrase.

Hang the letters on the wall using brass-plated hangers or other suitable framing hardware. Or position the letters on a shelf. ✄

SOURCES
iLovetoCreate provided the Collage Pauge Instant Decoupage: (800) 438-6226, ilovetocreate.com.
Jo-Ann Fabric and Craft Stores carries papier-mâché letters: (888) 739-4120, joann.com.

HAUTE
Hamper

{ by Shannon Dennis }

Disguise dirty laundry in a stylish
hamper featuring custom appliqués
and removable laundry bags.

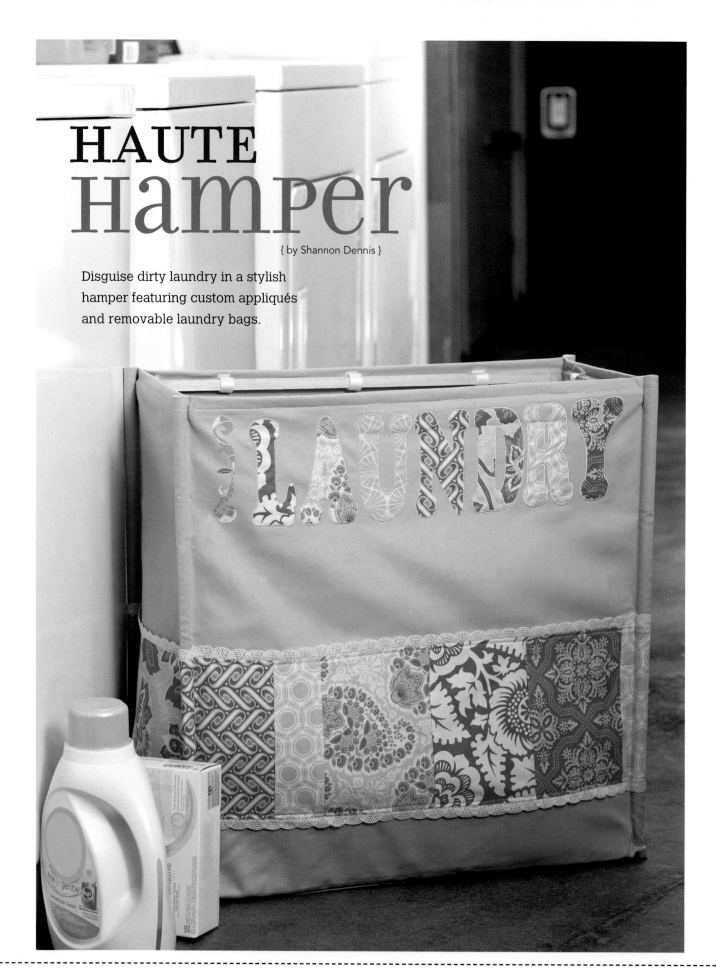

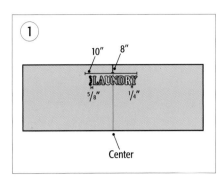

Supplies

Supplies listed are enough to make one 10½"x22"x23" hamper and two 20"x24" laundry bags.

- 3 yards of home-décor fabric (A)
- 1½ yards of coordinating solid cotton fabric (B)
- 1 yard each of two coordinating print cotton fabrics (C & D)
- ½ yard each of five coordinating print cotton fabrics (E, F, G, H & I)
- 1 yard of heavyweight double-sided stiff fusible interfacing
- Two 9"x12" sheets of fusible web
- 4 yards of 1"-wide lace trim
- 5½ yards of ¾"-wide satin ribbon
- 7"x22" rectangle of cut-away stabilizer
- Thread: all-purpose & decorative
- Hand sewing needle
- Removable fabric marker
- Ten ¼"-diameter snaps
- ½"-diameter wooden dowels: one 36"-long square, one 48"-long square & two 48"-long round
- Hand or table saw
- Wood glue
- Staple gun and staples

Cut

From fabric A, cut one 25"x71" rectangle for the hamper and one 11½"x24" rectangle for the hamper bottom.

From fabric B, cut two 11½"x24" rectangles for the hamper base and two 16½"x42" rectangles for the laundry bag lower panels.

Cut two 15½"x42" rectangles each from fabrics C and D for the laundry bag upper panels.

Cut three 6"x8" rectangles each from fabrics E, F, G and H for the band. From fabric I, cut four 3"x8" rectangles for the band. From fabrics E, F, G, H and I, cut a total of eight 4"x7" rectangles for the appliqués.

From the interfacing, cut one 11½"x24" rectangle.

From the lace trim, cut two 71"-long pieces.

From the ribbon, cut two 82"-long pieces and ten 2½"-long pieces for the frame loops.

From the 48"-long square dowel, cut two 24"-long pieces using a hand or table saw. From the two 48"-long round dowels, cut four 22"-long pieces. From the 36"-long square dowel, cut two 9"-long pieces.

Appliqué

Copy the appliqué letters and filigree templates from pages 38-39.

Adhere a piece of fusible web to each appliqué rectangle wrong side, following the manufacturer's instructions. Designate one appliqué rectangle for each appliqué letter and filigree, as desired.

Trace each letter and filigree template onto the corresponding appliqué rectangle paper backing. Carefully cut out each appliqué using small, sharp scissors. Remove the paper backing; set aside.

Fold the hamper rectangle in half widthwise to find the center; press, and then unfold. Position the hamper rectangle right side up on a flat work surface. Designate one rectangle long edge as the upper edge.

Measure 8" from the rectangle upper edge along the centerline; mark. Draw a 5"-long horizontal line from each side of the mark.

Position the letter N appliqué right side up over the hamper rectangle, aligning the upper edge with the horizontal line and the left edge with the center line; pin. Position the remaining letters on the hamper to spell out "Laundry," spacing the letters ¼" apart and aligning the upper edges with the horizontal line; pin.

Position the filigree appliqué right edge ⅝" from the letter L appliqué left edge; pin. Make sure the letters are evenly spaced and aligned. Once satisfied with the placement, remove the pins; fuse (1).

Select a narrow satin stitch and thread the machine with decorative thread. Center the stabilizer rectangle on the fabric wrong side under the appliqué letters. Satin stitch each appliqué perimeter. Remove the excess stabilizer beyond the appliqué perimeters, following the manufacturer's instructions.

Snap the loops together to secure the frame and hamper.

Construct

Use ¹/₂″ seam allowances unless otherwise noted.

Hamper

Select a straight stitch and thread the machine with all-purpose thread.

Fold the hamper rectangle upper edge 1″ toward the wrong side; press. Fold again 2″ toward the wrong side; press. Topstitch 1″ from the second fold.

With right sides together, stitch two large band rectangle long edges using a ¹/₄″ seam allowance. Press the seam toward the darker fabric. Repeat to stitch the remaining large and small band rectangles to form one strip.

With right sides together, align one lace trim and band long edge; stitch using a ¹/₄″ seam allowance. Fold the lace toward the band wrong side; press. Repeat to stitch the remaining lace trim to the opposite band long edge.

Position the hamper rectangle right side up on a flat work surface. Draw a straight horizontal line 8" from the rectangle lower edge. Position the band right side up over the hamper, aligning the band lower edge with the horizontal line; pin. Topstitch ¹/₄″ from each band long edge **(2)**.

With right sides together, stitch the hamper rectangle short ends using a 1″ seam allowance; press open the seam. Serge- or zigzag-finish the seams independently.

Position the hamper right side up on a flat work surface. Measure 13″ from each side of the center front and center back; pin-mark. Fold along one pin-mark with wrong sides together, matching the upper and lower edges. Stitch 1″ from the fold to create a dowel casing, ending the stitching 1″ from the hamper lower edge. Repeat to create the remaining three dowel casings.

Fold each hamper side in half lengthwise to find the center; press, and then unfold. Fold the hamper bottom in half lengthwise and widthwise to find the center; press, and then unfold.

With right sides together, pin the hamper-bottom perimeter to the hamper lower edges, matching each centerline. Stitch each long edge, beginning at one casing seam and ending at the opposite casing seam. Repeat to stitch each short edge. Stitch each casing corner. Turn the hamper right side out.

2

LAUNDRY

¹/₄″
¹/₄″
¹/₂″

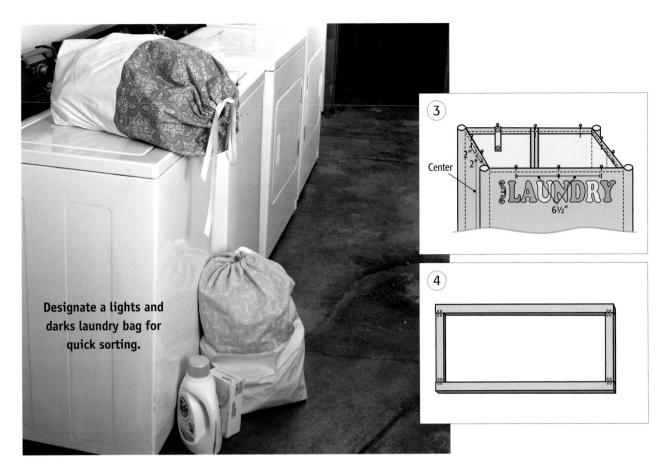

Designate a lights and darks laundry bag for quick sorting.

Position one hamper-base rectangle right side down on a flat work surface, and then center the interfacing rectangle over the hamper base. Position the remaining hamper-base rectangle right side up over the interfacing. Fuse the interfacing to the fabric layers, following the manufacturer's instructions. Serge- or zigzag-finish the hamper-base perimeter.

Pin-mark the hamper center front and back at the upper edge. Measure 6½″ from each side of the center mark; pin-mark. Measure 2″ from each side of the centerline on each hamper-side upper edge; pin-mark.

Center a female snap ¼″ from one frame-loop short end; hand stitch. With the wrong side facing up, center the opposite frame-loop short end on one hamper upper-edge pin; repin. Stitch 1″ from the upper edge to secure the frame loop. Center a male snap ¼″ from the stitched frame-loop short end; hand stitch **(3)**. Repeat to stitch the remaining frame loops along the remaining pin-marks.

On a flat work surface, align the two 24″-long dowels parallel and 9″ apart. Position each 9″-long dowel between the 24″-long dowel ends to create a rectangle. Secure the frame intersections using wood glue and staples; let dry **(4)**.

Place the frame into the hamper opening. Wrap each frame loop around the frame, and then snap the loops together. Insert one 22″-long dowel into each hamper casing. Insert the hamper base into the hamper bottom.

Laundry Bags

With right sides together, stitch the bag upper-panel lower edge to the bag lower-panel upper edge; press the seam toward the upper-panel. Topstitch the upper-panel ¼″ from the seam.

With right sides together, stitch the bag side; press open the seam. Serge- or zigzag-finish the seams independently. Fold the bag upper edge ½″ toward the wrong side; press, and then fold again 1″ toward the wrong side; press. Topstitch 1″ from the second fold to create a casing.

Stitch a ¼″-wide tacking stitch on the upper-edge fold at the bag side seam. Stitch another tacking stitch ⅞″ from the first tacking stitch at the bag side seam. Remove the seam stitching between the two tacking stitches. Using a safety pin, thread one ribbon length through the casing.

With right sides together, stitch the bag lower edge. To box the corners, align one side seam with the lower-edge seam. Measure 10″ from the corner; mark a horizontal line using a removable fabric marker. Stitch along the line. Trim off the corner.

Repeat to stitch the remaining laundry bag. ✄

SOURCES
Westminster Fibers provided home-décor fabric from the Decorator Solids by Amy Butler collection and print cotton fabric from the Heirloom by Joel Dewberry collection from Rowan Fabrics: (866) 907-3305, westminsterfibers.com

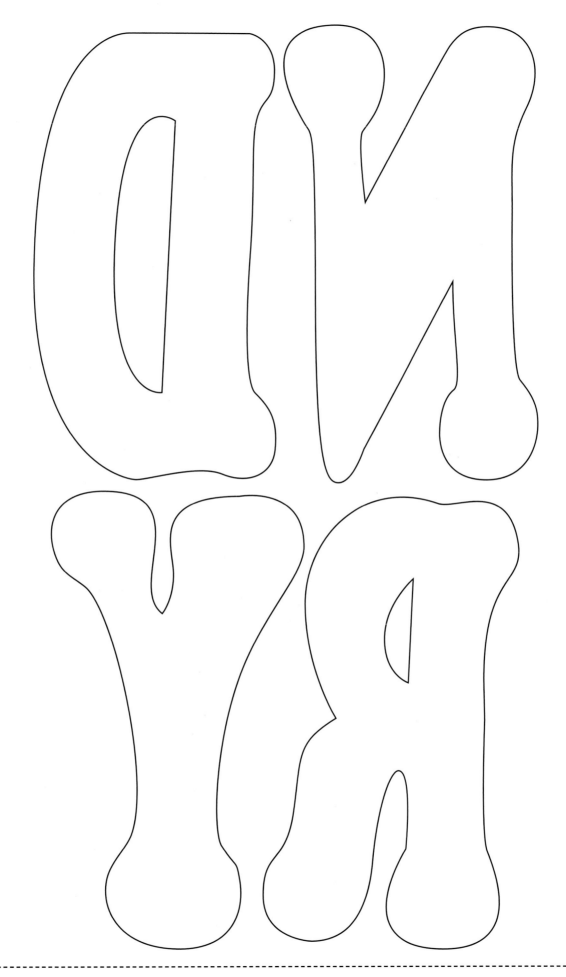

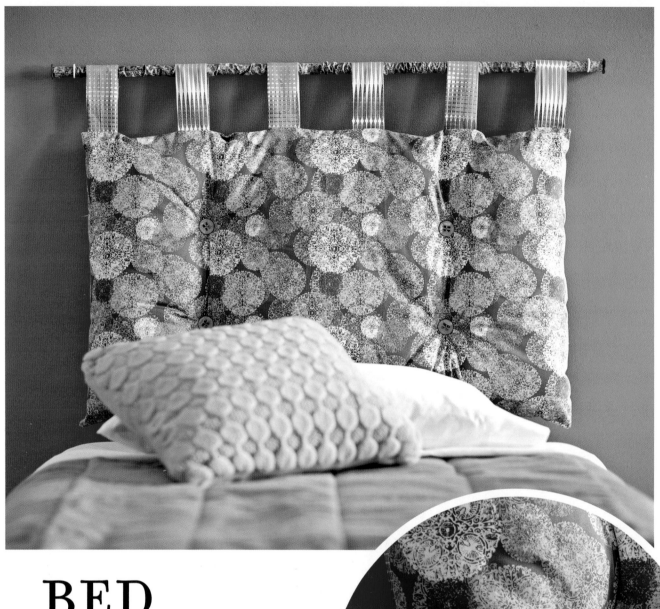

BED
HEAD

{ by Carol Zentgraf }

Dress up any bedroom with a custom-made reversible hanging headboard. It's cute to look at, comfy to lean on, and easy to coordinate with a bedspread or comforter. Hang it from a covered curtain rod strategically positioned over the bed.

Supplies

Supplies listed are enough to make one twin-size headboard measuring 24"x41".

- 1 yard each of two 54"-wide coordinating home-décor fabrics
- Polyester fiberfill
- Ten 1¼"-diameter buttons with holes
- ½"-diameter 44"-long curtain rod with finials removed
- Thread: coordinating all-purpose & waxed button
- Needles: 6"-long curved upholstery & hand sewing
- Removable fabric marker
- Permanent fabric adhesive

Tip: For king or queen sizes, consider creating two shorter headboards to hang side by side.

Cut

From each fabric, cut one 25" x 42" rectangle for the headboard panels.

Cut six 6" x 12" strips from one fabric for the tabs.

From the remaining fabric, cut one 3½" x 54" strip for the curtain rod casing.

Assemble

Use ½" seam allowances.

To create each tab, fold one strip in half lengthwise with right sides together. Stitch the long edges. Turn the tab right side out; press, centering the seam on the tab back. Fold each tab in half widthwise with the backs together.

Pin one tab to one panel upper edge, positioning the tab raw ends 1" from the panel left edge. Repeat to pin another tab 1" from the panel right edge. Evenly space the four remaining tabs between the outer tabs; pin **(1)**. Baste the tab ends to secure.

With right sides together, stitch the headboard panels along the perimeter, leaving a 4" opening along the lower edge for turning. Turn the panel right

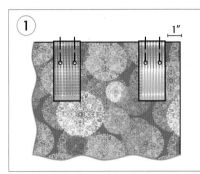

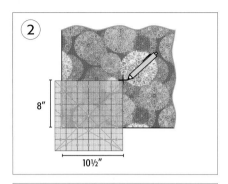

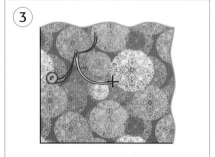

Turn the headboard around and switch out throw pillows for a quick décor update.

side out. Press, folding the opening edges toward the wrong side.

At each panel corner, measure 10½″ from the short edge and 8″ from the long edge; mark using a removable fabric marker (2).

Stuff the headboard panels with polyester fiberfill, and then slipstitch the opening closed.

Cut a 9″ length of waxed button thread. Slide the thread ends through the holes of one button from the front to the back. Thread the upholstery needle with both thread ends and stitch through one placement mark on the headboard front (3). Bring the needle out through the corresponding mark on the headboard back. Remove the needle and tie the thread ends through the holes of a second button. Knot

the thread ends together several times, pulling tightly to tuft the headboard. Repeat to stitch the three remaining button sets.

Fold the curtain rod casing in half lengthwise with right sides together. Stitch the long edge, and then turn right side out; press. Apply a small amount of permanent fabric adhesive inside each curtain rod end, and then tuck the fabric ends into the rod. Let the glue dry before adding the finials.

To create the button finials, cut a 3-yard length of waxed button thread. Insert the ends through one button from the right side. Thread the upholstery needle with the thread ends, and then knot the ends around the needle eye. Drop the threaded needle through one rod end and out of the

opposite end. Remove the needle and tie the remaining button securely in place. Clip the thread ends 2″ from the knot and insert them inside the tube. Apply a small amount of fabric adhesive to each rod end under the button to keep it centered.

Slide the rod through the tabs and hang the headboard on the wall above the bed. ✂

SOURCES

Fairfield Processing Corp. provided the Poly-Fil fiberfill: (800) 980-8000, fairfieldworld.com.

JHB provided the buttons, #40156 and #40153: (800) 525-9007, buttons.com.

Prym Consumer USA provided the waxed button thread and upholstery needle: dritz.com.

Westminster Fibers provided the Ty Pennington Impressions fabric collection: (866) 907-3305, westminsterfibers.com.

COOL
{ by Lynne Farris }
canopies

A canopy is a beautiful design element that becomes the focal point of a room's décor.

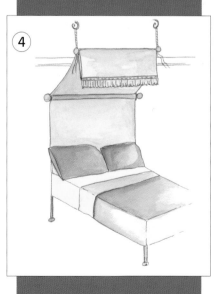

Originally, bed canopies were functional draping used to provide privacy, protect the sleeper from cold drafts or to deter mosquitoes. Today, canopies serve as decorative elements, allowing myriad style options. Style choices, including color, fabric, weight, pattern, texture and construction, can transform the look of a room. These elements make a room masculine or feminine, traditional or contemporary, casual or formal or simple or opulent.

There are several canopy styles, each based on a standard canopy bed frame. Using the canopy designs at right for inspiration, measure the bed and canopy frame to estimate the amount of fabric needed. If using print fabrics, line the canopy to achieve a professionally finished look. Home-décor width fabrics work to cover child, twin and double bed canopies; however, when working with queen and king beds, plan strategically placed seams to achieve a polished look. Colorful sheets in coordinated prints and solids offer economical options when wider fabric widths are needed.

Design Options
CRISP & CLEAN (1)
This style works well with crisp solids, such as linen, silk taffeta or heavyweight cottons. The canopy features a single pleat in each panel center to maintain a tailored, formal look. There are also full-length gathered drapes at each corner and across the headboard width. Create simple fabric tiebacks to secure the drapes to the bed posts. Pair this canopy with square flange pillow covers, tailored bolsters and fitted bed covers for an upscale style, a masculine look or a lavish guest retreat.

GRANDIOSE & GORGEOUS (2)
Use a summery eyelet, colorful stripes or a floral print to create this frilly, whimsical ensemble. This design is perfect for a young girl's room, as it features the softened look of gathered panels that are edged with a generous frosting of ruffles or trim. Add fluffy pillows, a thick quilted duvet and a billowy dust ruffle.

SOFT & FLOWY (3)
Create an airy coastal look with minimum effort by draping generous panels of gauzy sheer fabric casually over a canopy frame. Secure the fabric by looping a piece of sheer fabric onto the frame in a single loose knot.

SIMPLE & MODERN (4)
This is a simple, inexpensive canopy design. Drape a length of finished fabric over two strategically placed curtain rods attached to the wall and ceiling to create the headboard and awning-like canopy. As a final touch, add binding or decorative fringe to finish the canopy edge. ✄

DIY
Duvets

{ by Ellen March }

Choose from three duvet styles to transform your bedroom.

A duvet cover can be a costly addition to a bedroom makeover. Sewing one yourself is not only cost-effective, but also allows your creativity to take center stage. To make things even easier, purchase two flat sheets the size of your duvet as opposed to buying fabric yardage. Then follow the instructions without the work of measuring and cutting.

Matching Motifs

Most fabrics require piecing to achieve the desired duvet width. Unless you choose very wide fabric, you'll need to match the pattern motif when piecing for a look that's pleasing to the eye.

Measure the distance between repeating designs along the selvage edge (1). This is the pattern repeat distance measurement for the formula below. You may lose a considerable amount of fabric (up to 10″ per fabric width) when aligning the motifs. Use the extra fabric to sew pillow sham accents, curtain borders, fabric-covered picture frames and more.

To join fabric widths, don't stitch the panels together with the seam running through the duvet center. Instead, cut one fabric width in half lengthwise and stitch the half panels to either side of the center panel for symmetry (2).

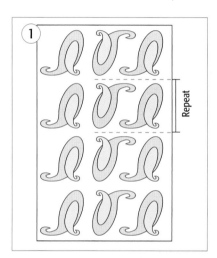

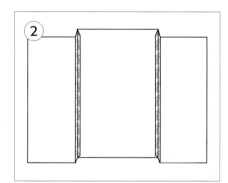

Button Duvet

All seams are ¹/₂″ unless otherwise noted.

The featured duvet cover was made for a queen-size comforter using 59″-wide fabric. Preshrink all fabrics prior to construction.

Supplies

- Fabric (according to duvet dimensions)
- Backing fabric (according to duvet dimensions)
- Six buttons (at least 1¹/₂″ diameter)
- Matching all-purpose thread

Cut the backing fabric to the duvet dimensions (a and b on "Duvet Dimensions" chart). If necessary, piece together fabric widths to achieve the desired dimensions.

Cut two fabric panels to the duvet width, plus 3″. Cut one panel to measure two thirds of the duvet length plus 7″ (upper panel) and cut one panel to measure one third of the duvet length plus 7″ (lower panel). Or piece together fabric to achieve the desired dimensions.

> **Tip:** When leaving the selvage on the fabric, clip the selvage every 4″ so the fabric doesn't pull up and pucker when washed.

DUVET DIMENSIONS

Take the following measurements of your existing comforter to calculate the fabric yardage needed.

- **Duvet width** (across bed from side to side) plus 3″ = _____(a)
- **Duvet length** (bed head to bed foot) plus 3″ = _____(b)
- **Fabric width** minus 4″ = _____(c)
- **Pattern repeat distance** (if applicable) = _____(d)
- **Add b + d** for fabric cut length = _____(e)
- **Divide a by c** (round to nearest whole number) for fabric cut width = _____(f)
- **Multiply e x f** = _____(g)
- **Divide g by 36** for required yardage (for one side of duvet cover) = _____fabric yards

Tip: Coordinate your bedroom décor. Freehand draw a design similar to your duvet fabric motif and copy it onto an artist's canvas. Paint the canvas and let dry. Hang the painting over your bed for a delightful designer detail.

Fold the upper-panel selvage edge 6″ toward the wrong side and press. Stitch close to the selvage edge. Stitch six horizontal buttonholes equidistant from each other 1″ from the folded edge **(3)**.

Zigzag-finish one long edge of the lower panel. Place the upper panel buttonhole edge over the lower panel zigzagged edge. (Make sure the lower panel upper edge extends beyond the buttonholes.) Pin the overlapped edges in place; stitch **(4)**. Using the buttonholes as a guide, pin-mark the button placements on the lower panel right side. Hand stitch the buttons in place and button through the buttonholes.

With right sides together, place the backing over the joined fabric panels. Align all corners and pin the perimeter; stitch.

Unbutton the buttons and turn the duvet right side out through the button opening; press. Topstitch the duvet perimeter close to the edge. Insert the comforter, matching the corners, and button the cover to close.

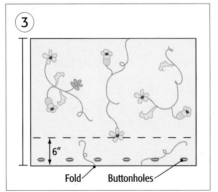

3

Fold   Buttonholes

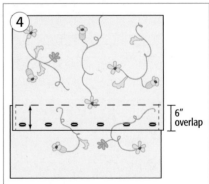

4

6″ overlap

Ribbon Duvet

All seams are ¹/₂″ unless otherwise noted.

The featured duvet cover was made for a king-size comforter using 45″-wide fabric. Preshrink all fabric prior to construction.

Supplies

- **Fabric (according to duvet dimensions)**
- **Backing fabric (according to duvet dimensions)**
- **1″-wide matching grosgrain ribbon (approximately 10 yards depending on duvet measurements)**
- **Fusible seam tape (such as Steam-A-Seam)**
- **Seam sealant (such as Fray Check)**
- **Matching all-purpose thread**

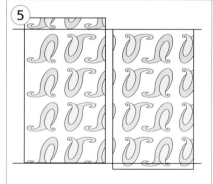

Cut the backing fabric to the duvet dimensions, adding 3″ to the length and width. If necessary, piece together fabric to achieve the desired dimensions.

Cut fabric panels to the duvet length, plus 3″. Align the fabric widths right side up on a flat surface, matching the

motif repeat if necessary **(5)**. Right sides together, stitch the panel long edges. Zigzag-finish and press open the seams. Trim any excess fabric if necessary.

Fold the fabric and backing lower edge ¹/₂″ to the wrong side and press.

Cut ribbon lengths to the duvet length, plus 3″. Cut as many ribbon lengths as there are panel seams. Fuse the seam tape to the ribbon wrong side following the manufacturer's instructions. Fuse the ribbon to the fabric right side along the seamlines. Topstitch the ribbon in place.

Cut twenty 8″ lengths of ribbon. On the fabric right side along the folded

Tip: Always purchase extra fabric when aligning patterns or motifs.

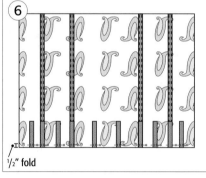

6

¹/₂" fold

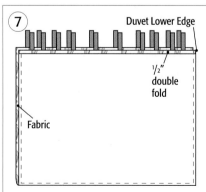

7

Duvet Lower Edge

¹/₂" double fold

Fabric

Tip: Use leftover fabric and trim to create coordinating pillows, shams, curtains and more.

lower edge, pin 10 ribbon short ends equidistant from each other **(6).** Topstitch the ribbons in place. Fold the fabric lower edge another ¹/₂" toward the wrong side and press. Topstitch close to the second fold. Knot the ribbon ends and, if desired, apply seam sealant to the raw edges to prevent fraying.

Repeat to stitch the remaining ribbons to the backing right side lower edge.

Right sides together and aligning all corners and ribbons, generously pin the backing to the duvet fabric. Stitch, leaving the lower edge open **(7).** Turn the duvet cover right side out. Insert a comforter into the duvet cover, matching the corners, and knot the ribbons to close the lower edge.

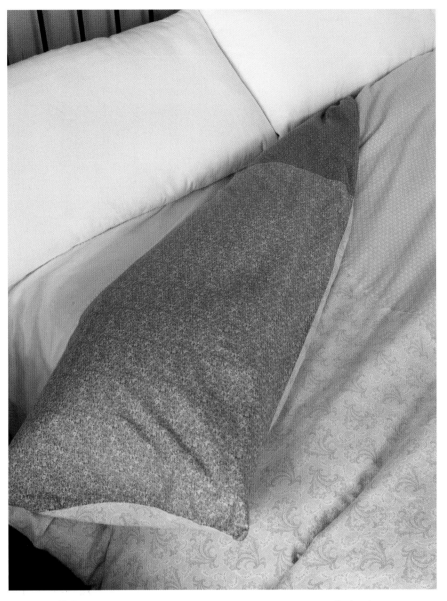

Reversible Duvet

Change your duvet cover with the seasons by using summer colors on one side and fall colors on the other. Turn the duvet cover over for a quick update.

To make the featured duvet cover, stitch 20 fabric tubes measuring 1"x 7"; leave an opening along one long edge for turning (8). Topstitch the tie perimeters, closing the openings with the stitches. Knot one short end of each tie. Stitch the opposite tie edges to the fabric and lining as directed for the ribbons (see figure 7 on the opposite page). Finish the duvet cover as instructed for the ribbon duvet. ✃

SOURCES

Fabrics-store.com, provided the 59"-wide Oasis Summer Ivy Print fabric for the button duvet on page 46: fabrics-store.com.

Fat Quarter Shop, carries 108"-wide fabrics: fatquartershop.com.

FreeSpirit, provided the Amy Butler Charm Spiced Mod Paisley fabric for the ribbon duvet on page 47: freespiritfabric.com.

Homespun Fabrics & Draperies, carries 100"- to 118"-wide fabrics: homespunfabrics.com.

Organic Cotton Plus, provided the 233 thread count 113"-wide organic cotton sateen sheeting for the ribbon and button duvet linings: organiccottonplus.com.

Warehouse Fabrics, Inc., carries 90"-wide quilting fabrics: warehousefabricsinc.com.

GO ORGANIC

Organic cotton fabric is a great choice for bedding. Not only is it softer to the touch than conventionally grown cotton, but it's also available in 100"- to 113"-wide sateen sheeting. The thread count ranges from 233 to 440, while the thread count of conventional cotton fabric ranges from 180 to 360. By choosing organically grown cotton you'll do a great service to our planet because organic cotton is grown with natural fertilizers and is free from toxic chemicals. Allergy-prone individuals and people with sensitive skin especially benefit from bedding made of organic cotton. So go organic and contribute to a healthier you and a healthier planet. Visit aboutorganiccotton.org for more information.

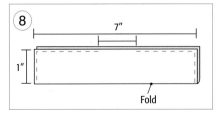

8

7"

1"

Fold

WONDERFUL
WINDOWS

{ by Lynne Farris }

Window treatments serve as a bridge between the architecture of a house and the furnishing style, making them important design and decorating elements.

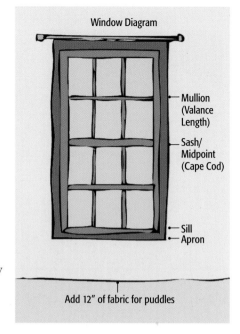

Window Diagram

Mullion (Valance Length)

Sash/ Midpoint (Cape Cod)

Sill
Apron

Add 12" of fabric for puddles

Window treatments are also functional, as they can be used to frame a lovely view, camouflage an unsightly scene, create privacy or mitigate effects of extreme heat or cold. Consider the purpose of the room in which the window is located. In a bedroom, draperies could be used to block out the sun; in a living room, more natural light is often desired. Also consider the amount of direct sunlight at various times of the day, the view, privacy issues and the overall appearance.

What's Your Style?

Use draperies to carry a color scheme, add texture or tie together various furnishings. Modify the following styles to suit any room décor.

Soft & Airy

Casually drape a single length of gauzy fabric over a plain curtain rod. Adjust the fabric to let in more or less natural light. This style is suitable for a living room or main foyer (1).

Formal & Dramatic

Using a single length of heavyweight fabric, such as velvet or silk, create swags along the curtain rod. This treatment adds elegance to a formal room (2).

Simple & Clean

Make tab-top curtains using drapery fabric in conjunction with blinds or shades to control light and privacy.

This informal treatment is great for bedrooms because it allows you to block out the sun when necessary (3).

Café Chic

Create a valance for the window upper edge and café-style curtains for the window lower edge. For a quick-and-easy makeover, create the valance from a square tablecloth corner and the café curtains from patterned bed sheets. Café-style curtains begin at the window midpoint and cover only the lower section. (See the Window Diagram above for placement.) This treatment is perfect for kitchens and dining rooms because it provides privacy and allows natural light to shine through (4).

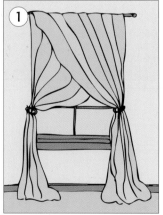

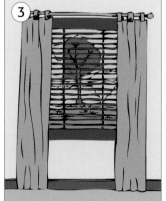

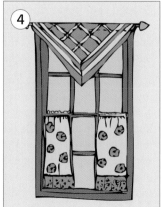

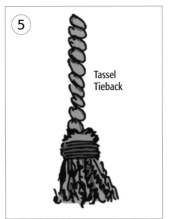
Tassel Tieback

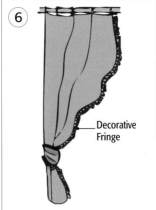
Decorative Fringe

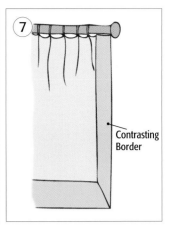
Contrasting Border

Length Matters

The drapery length affects the overall appearance of the room. There are four primary drapery lengths: the sill, the apron and the floor or "puddles."

THE SILL

Short curtains suit an informal room. Use this length when creating a café-style curtain.

THE APRON

This area of the window, just below the sill, is a great length for an informal window treatment.

THE FLOOR

Make sure the draperies graze the floor. They look messy if they end just above the floor or over the molding upper edge.

PUDDLES

For a romantic and formal look, create puddle panels that gather on the floor.

Fabric Selection

Select a fabric that appropriately accommodates the desired design. For example, choose sheer, loosely woven muslin for a soft look that allows for lots of natural light. Or choose heavily patterned silk to add elegance to the room. Linen damask and thick velvet create a dramatic appearance and also block out natural light.

Use linings and interlinings to adjust the weight, drape and amount of light transmitted through the main fabric. Linings also unify the look of your window treatments from the outside,

positively affecting the curb appeal of your home.

Measure Twice

Before beginning, measure the window height and width; record. Measure the area surrounding the window, keeping in mind that the curtain and rod extends beyond the window dimensions. Generally, the curtain rod sits approximately 5″ to 6″ above the window upper edge; adjust the rod position based on personal preference. Consider the amount of fabric needed based on the window measurements and the amount of extra fabric needed along the window perimeter. Draperies usually extend 2″ to 3″ beyond the window sides. Additionally, consider how much extra fabric is necessary to accommodate pleats, gathers, hems, casings and extra length, if using tiebacks.

Cut Once

Prepare the sewing area. You'll need a yardstick, tape measure, heavyweight shears and a rotary cutting system for best results. Use a large cutting table to accommodate the large fabric panels. Purchase extra fabric length and width.

Pressing Matter

When constructing window treatments, carefully and accurately press before and after sewing each seam to ensure professional results. Use a large ironing surface, such as a padded worktable, along with a high-quality steam iron and

press cloth. Check the fabric content before applying heat or water, and set the iron to the appropriate heat setting.

Finishing Touch

These functional and decorative elements provide the finishing touches that give your window treatment a professional designer look:

RODS AND HANGING HARDWARE

Consider the overall style when selecting a curtain rod. Make sure the rod supports the fabric style and weight.

TIEBACKS

Select a tieback as simple as a plain cord that's looped around one panel and attached to the wall by a small cup hook. Or choose a tieback that stands as the focal point of the treatment, such as a fringe cord.

TASSELS

Tie or stitch tassels to the tiebacks to add a fun focal point to the window treatment (5).

DECORATIVE TRIM

Add decorative trim to each curtain panel perimeter to enhance the overall appearance (6).

BORDERS

Stitch a contrasting border on each curtain panel for a dramatic and interesting effect. For example, if using white fabric for the curtain, attach a colored border to match the room décor and really make the curtains stand out (7). ✁

HOME DEC
PLeaTs

{ by Carol Zentgraf }

Whether you're making floor-length draperies, sill-length curtains or a valance, pleats add a designer touch and offer countless creative options. Learn about different pleat types, fool-proof measuring methods and products to make pleats quickly and accurately.

Pleat Styles

Box pleats have two folds that face away from each other on the right side and toward each other on the wrong side. An inverted box pleat is basically a box pleat created upside down so that the "box" appears on the fabric wrong side.

The inverted box pleat offers a number of creative options and is ideal for valances. Add a single center pleat and corner pleats or two single pleats evenly spaced from the valance center. Both pleat types unify a room because they are subtle and complementary to existing room décor. They are suitable for bed skirts, ottomans, slipcovers and table skirts.

Create shallow pleats spaced 3″ apart or deep pleats space 6″ or wider apart. Hang closely spaced pleats with rings, drapery hooks, tabs or a board mount. Curtains with widely spaced pleats are best hung with clip-on rings, a rod pocket, tabs or a board mount.

Consider the valance height and width and keep the pleat size proportionate. Wider pleats are suitable for a treatment with a minimal number of accent pleats.

To determine the pleat allowance, select the inverted pleat width and multiply by two. Choose a narrow 1″-wide pleat for lightweight or sheer fabrics, or up to 8″-wide pleats for mediumweight fabrics.

Use pins to mark the pleat allowances and spacing along the curtain upper-edge right side, according to the determined measurements (1).

Fold the pleat allowance pins to meet at the center point; pin, and then press (2). Baste the upper edge through the pleat layers.

BOX PLEAT

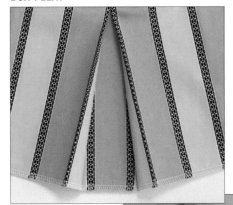

PINCH PLEATS

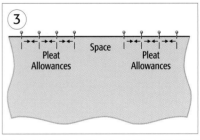

3 Pinch   2 Pinch

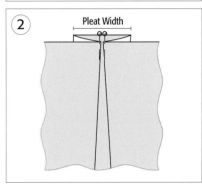

GOBLET PLEAT

Tip: Adjust the pleat foldlines on even vertical stripe fabric to create a unique stripe sequence.

If desired, piece the curtain using contrasting fabric for the pleat allowances. Tack the corners back and hand stitch buttons on each corner edge. Add an embroidery design to the inverted pleat.

Pinch pleats, also called French pleats, are classic pleats that can be used for window treatments in any room of the house. They are typically made with two or three $\frac{5}{8}''$ to $1''$-wide pleats, spaced $3''$ to $4''$ apart.

To determine the pleat allowance, select the pinch pleat width, multiply by two, and then multiply by the desired number of pinch pleats. For example, for a $1''$-wide triple pinch pleat, the total pleat allowance is $6''$.

Use pins to mark the pleat allowances and spacing across the curtain upper-edge right side, according to the determined measurements (3).

Fold the upper edge to abut the pleat allowance pins, creating three consecutive pleats; pin. Stitch parallel to the pleat fold from the curtain upper edge to the header lower edge. Tack the pleats together at the curtain upper edge and the pleat fronts at the header lower edge (4). Repeat to create each pinch pleat.

For easier spacing, stitch curtain tape to the header. Curtain tape has double or triple pockets that easily form pleats when pinch pleat hooks are added to

the pockets. Attach drapery hooks to each pleat wrong side, and then hang.

Goblet pleats are constructed in the same manner as pinch pleats, but without individual smaller pleats. Hang goblet pleats with drapery hooks attached to each pleat wrong side.

A standard goblet pleat allowance is $6''$ to $7''$-wide, although it can be narrower for short curtains or lightweight fabrics.

To determine the pleat allowance, select the goblet pleat width, and then multiply by two.

Use pins to mark the pleat allowances and spacing along the curtain upper-edge right side, according to the determined measurements.

① Pleat Allowance   Space   Pleat Allowance

② Pleat Width

③ Pleat Allowances   Space   Pleat Allowances

④

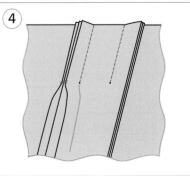

DIAMOND PLEATS

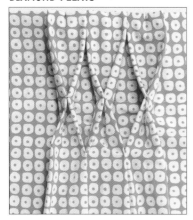

PENCIL PLEATS

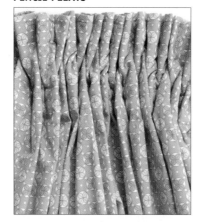

SMOCKING PLEATS

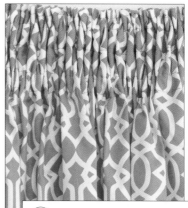

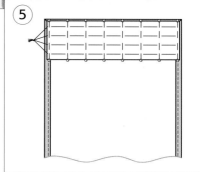

Fold the upper edge to abut the pleat-allowance pins; pin. Stitch parallel to the pleat fold from the curtain upper edge to the header lower edge. Gather each pleat at the header lower edge; stitch, wrapping the thread tightly to create a pinched base. Lightly stuff the pleats with fiberfill. Repeat to create the remaining goblet pleats.

If desired, cover buttons with matching or contrasting fabric and stitch to each pleat base. Add a tassel to each button or connect the buttons with draped cording.

Diamond pleats are double pinch pleats with the upper and lower pleat edges tacked together to create a diamond effect.

Use pins to mark 4″-wide pleat allowances spaced 2″ apart along the curtain upper edge. Pin-mark the pleat allowance centers.

Fold the upper edge to abut the pleat allowance pins, creating two consecutive pleats; pin. Stitch parallel to the pleat fold from the curtain upper edge to the header lower edge. Repeat to create the remaining double pleats.

To create the diamond shape, tack the upper-right pleat corner to the adjacent upper-left pleat corner. Repeat to tack the remaining pleat corners. Tack together the pleat folds 3″ to 4″

below the header lower edge. Repeat to tack the remaining pleats.

Pencil pleats are long, narrow, closely spaced pleats. They create a very full decorative curtain. Broken pencil pleats are a variation with a similar appearance, but the pleats are long and misaligned or "broken" rather than straight. Use curtain tape with pull cords to create pencil pleats. Both types are best for long, casual window treatments.

Cut a curtain tape length several inches longer than the header length. Place the curtain tape on a flat work surface with the cord side up and the colored line along the upper edge.

Cut one tape short end and pull the cords out of the tape 2″ from the cut end. Trim the tape ½″ from the cords, and then fold the tape edge toward the wrong side. Place the tape on the header, aligning the folded end with the side edge; pin. Trim the remaining tape end and fold the edge toward the wrong side **(5)**.

Stitch the tape to the header along both side edges and between the cords, being careful not to catch the cords in the stitching. Pull the cords on the upper edge and knot the ends. Gently pull the cords from the opposite edge until the tape and header are completely gathered and the cords are no longer

visible, making sure there's no puckering. Knot the cord ends close to the last pleat, and then knot the cord ends together, leaving long tails, allowing them to be laundered flat. Hang the curtain on a rod with hooks.

Smocking pleats feature an intricate series of straight, shallow and evenly spaced pleats with a smocked appearance. They create fullness best suited for casual full-length window treatments. Use curtain tape with pull cords to create smocking pleats. Follow the pencil pleat instructions to apply the tape, making sure they're evenly spaced with larger pleat allowances.

Measure

Accurate measuring and marking is essential for uniform pleated window treatments. Take time to properly measure the window and determine the number of panel(s) needed and the pleat treatment desired.

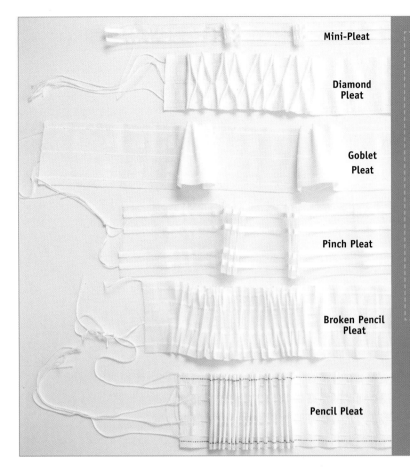

Mini-Pleat

Diamond Pleat

Goblet Pleat

Pinch Pleat

Broken Pencil Pleat

Pencil Pleat

CURTAIN TAPE 101

Using curtain tapes with cords is a quick and easy way to make pleats for window treatments, such as pencil pleats or smocking pleats, which would otherwise be a time-consuming task by hand. The tapes don't permanently stitch the pleats, allowing the cords to be released and the curtain to be washed or dry cleaned flat.

The tapes are sold on a bolt and labeled with the curtain fullness, which helps determine how much fabric and tape is needed for the curtain width. All tapes are applied in the same manner (see Pencil Pleats at left for application instructions).

Tip: Pleats retain their shape and look the best with crinoline, buckram or heading tape for all pleat styles except box pleats because they don't require extra stability.

Measure the window height and width; record. Multiply the original width measurement by $2\frac{1}{2}$ to 3 to account for the drapery fullness.

To determine the number of pleats, allow for any return or overlap and plan a pleat at the corner of each return or just before the overlap. For a curtain with corner pleats, evenly space the pleats between the corners. For a flat curtain, pleat 2″ from each side edge and evenly space the remaining pleats between the outer pleats. The pleat allowance depends on the pleat style selected, usually from 4″ to 6″.

To determine the cut width, multiply the determined number of pleats by the pleat allowance for the total pleat allowance. For example, for five 4″-wide pleats, the total pleat allowance is 20″. Add the total pleat allowance and side-edge hem allowances to the finished curtain width for the total cut width.

To determine the cut height for a double header, add 6″ to 8″ to the recorded height measurement plus the desired hem allowance.

To determine the cut height for a box pleat curtain, add the desired hem allowance plus 4″ for a header if it will be hung from a rod with hooks, $\frac{1}{2}$″ for a rod pocket or tabs, or a 2″ overlap allowance for a board mount.

Construct

From the curtain fabric, cut the panel(s) according to the desired pleat measurements.

Construct the curtain, lining the curtain if desired. For full-length drapes, finish the header with pleats, and then hang to mark for hemming. For valances and shorter curtains, hem the curtain before finishing the header with pleats.

To prepare the header for pleats, fold the upper edge $\frac{1}{2}$″ toward the wrong side; press. Fold again 3″ to 4″ to the wrong side; press, and then stitch close to the first fold.

If applicable, stitch a 3″ to 4″-wide strip of crinoline, buckram or heading tape between the two heading layers.

RESOURCE
Inverted box pleat valance from Machine Embroidery Room-by-Room by Carol Zentgraf, Krause Publications.

SOURCES
Michael Miller Fabrics provided the fabric for the inverted box pleat, pinch pleat, diamond pleat broken pencil pleat and smocking pleat samples: (212)704-0774, michaelmillerfabrics.com.
Waverly Fabrics provided the fabric for the inverted box pleat valance and goblet pleat samples: waverly.com.
Wrights provided the Magic Curtain Tapes: (877) 597-4448, wrights.com.

MADE IN THE
SHADE

{ by Pam Damour }

Making Roman shades doesn't have to be
a daunting task. Once you find the correct
supplies, you can quickly and easily update
your décor with custom window treatments.

Supplies

- **Main fabric & lining** (amount according to measurements)
- **Carpenter's square** or square ruler
- **Thread:** all-purpose & invisible (optional)
- **3/8"-diameter plastic ribs** (amount & length according to shade measurements; see "Sources.")
- **3/8"-diameter metal weight bar** (1/2" shorter than shade width; see "Sources.")
- **3/8"-diameter plastic or metal rings** (amount determined by shade size; see "Sources.")
- **Wooden mounting board**
- **Cord lock or pulley**
- **Lift cord**
- **Screw eyes**
- **Lift cord adjusters**
- **Cord tassel**
- **Staple gun & staples**
- **Removable fabric marker**
- **Ring-attaching gun** (optional; see "Sources.")
- **Edge-joining and appliqué feet** (optional)
- **Cord reel** (optional)

Measure

To determine the main fabric width, measure the window width and add 2"; record.

To determine the main fabric length, measure the window length and add 10"; record. For an outside mount (see "Mounting Matters" on page 61), add 4" to the recorded measurement.

To determine the lining width, measure the window width: record.

To determine the lining length, measure the window length and add 10"; record. For an outside mount, add 4" to the recorded measurement.

Tip: Often plaids are not suitable for Roman shades, especially if the plaid is uneven.

To add a permanent fold at the shade lower edge, add 8" to the recorded length measurements.

Cut

Cut the fabric and lining pieces according to the recorded measurements. Use a carpenter's square to cut exact 90° corners. It's more important to cut the fabric on the square than on the straight of grain.

From remaining lining fabric, cut a strip 1"x the shade width to make a sleeve for the weight bar.

Construct

Use 1/2" seam allowances unless otherwise noted.

Position the fabric and lining pieces with right sides together, aligning one side edge; stitch. Align the opposite

edge; stitch. Press the seam allowances toward the fabric.

Turn the shade right side out. Press the side edges so that 1/2" of fabric folds toward the lining side.

Designate one short edge as the lower edge. Double-fold the lower edge 4" toward the lining side; press, and then pin (1).

Thread the machine with invisible thread. If desired, install an edge-joining foot. Stitch close to the first folded edge through all layers (2).

With the lining side facing up, mark the ring locations. Beginning 1/2" from one side edge, mark the stitched fold every 12". Repeat to mark ring locations 8" above the first marked row. Repeat to mark ring locations on the entire shade.

Pin through all layers at each mark. Thread a hand sewing needle with invisible thread. Hand stitch a ring at each mark.

Or set the machine to a wide zigzag stitch and lower the feed dogs. Install an appliqué foot or remove the presser foot. Position one ring edge over the mark; remove the pin. Stitch the ring in place through all layers, making sure the needle clears the edges (3). Repeat to stitch a ring at each mark.

If using a ring-attaching gun, first hand or machine stitch the rings along the hem fold, as they'll experience the most stress during use. Push the needle through the fabric at each mark from the lining side (4). Hold the fabric firmly, and then squeeze the trigger until the ring shoots onto the fabric and the plastic "T" pops out on the other side (5).

Cut each plastic rib ¼" shorter than the shade width. Insert the first rib through the shade upper opening, and then slide it down to rest on the first ring row. Repeat to place a rib above each remaining ring row.

Fold the weight-bar sleeve strip in half lengthwise. Stitch one long edge. Turn the tube right side out, and then insert the weight bar into the sleeve opening (6).

Insert the weight bar into the shade lower casing. Hand stitch the side openings closed (7).

Prepare for Mounting

Use leftover lining fabric to wrap the mounting board; staple the fabric in place (8).

If the board edges will be visible after mounting, fold a scrap of fabric around each end; staple (9). Fold the fabric raw edges toward the board back; staple (10).

Determine the desired side for the pull cord. Attach the pulley or cord lock to the mounting board 2" from the desired side edge, following the manufacturer's instructions (11).

Align the mounting board with the shade upper edge. Mark the mounting board above each column of rings. Insert a screw eye at each mark, either by predrilling holes or using a bit designed to install screw eyes (12). If the screen is very large, install a pulley at each mark instead of a screw eye.

Using a removable fabric marker or crayon, draw a line 2" below and parallel to the screen upper edge to indicate the finished upper edge.

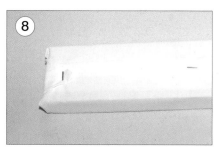

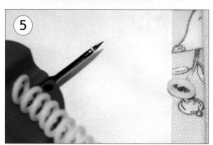

Tip: After constructing the shade, create crisp folds in the fabric before mounting. Fold the shade as it will be folded when drawn open. Loosely tie fabric strips around the shade and allow it set overnight. Steam if desired.

Wrap the shade upper edge around the mounting board, aligning the marked line with the mounting board upper edge. Staple the excess shade fabric in place (13).

String the Shade

To add a permanent lower fold, thread the cord through the cord adjuster, and then through the two lowest rings below the pulley. Thread the cord back through the adjuster. Knot the cord end and pull tight to bring the two rings together and form the fold (14).

If omitting the lower fold, first thread the cord through the adjuster, and then through the lowest ring. Thread the cord back through the adjuster; knot the cord end.

Continue feeding the cord through each ring until you reach the screw eye. Thread the cord through the screw eye, and then through the inner pulley slot, leaving about 3' of excess cord hanging free.

String the second cord through the second row of rings, and then through the appropriate screw eye and pulley slot. Cut the cord end to match the first cord length below the pulley. Repeat the process to thread cord through the remaining ring rows (15).

Pull the cords together below the pulley to achieve even tension. Tie the cords in an overhand knot below the pulley. Evenly trim the cord ends to the desired length.

Braid the cords from the knot to the ends to create the shade pull. Tie the ends to a cord reel or tie in another overhand knot (16).

Mount

For an inside mount, place the shade inside the window so the mounting board front is flush with the window opening edge. Using a 1³/₄″ screw, screw through the mounting board and into the window frame.

For an outside mount, draw a line 4″ above the window. Align the mounting board upper edge with the line, centering the shade over the window. Using 2″ screws, screw through the mounting board about 2″ from each end and into the wall. Note that windows have a header board above the upper edge inside the wall, so finding a stud shouldn't be a problem. If you don't find a stud, reinforce the holes with a drywall anchor. ✁

SOURCES
Pam Damour carries supplies for making Roman shades: 518-297-2699, pamdamour.com.
Virginia Aardvark, LLC carries a ring-attaching gun: vaaardvark.com.

MOUNTING MATTERS

Follow these steps to successfully mount the Roman shade.

- **Determine** whether to mount the shade inside or outside of the window frame.

- **For an inside mount,** the mounting board is installed flat inside the window frame upper edge. The shade hardware is installed on the mounting board back **(A)**.

- **For an outside mount,** the mounting board is installed on the wall above the window or door, so the hardware is attached to the board narrow lower edge **(B)**. To allow the hardware to operate correctly, the shade should extend ½″ beyond the window side edges and 4″ above the window upper edge.

- **At the lumber store,** look for a 1'x2' yellow pine board to mount the shade. If the store doesn't carry 1'x2' boards, purchase a 1'x4' board and have it cut lengthwise (also known as "ripping the board").

- **For an outside mount,** cut the board length to the finished shade width measurement.

- **For an inside mount,** cut the board length ¼″ shorter than the window opening width.

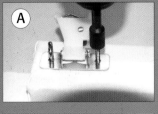

Use small fabric scraps to stitch a cute collection of picnic weights to prevent napkins and tablecloths from blowing away in the summer breeze.

ANIMAL Farm

{ by Lucy Blaire }

Supplies

- Assorted fabric and lining scraps (at least 4½" square)
- All-purpose thread
- Vinyl scraps (at least 3" square)
- Polyester fiberfill
- Embroidery floss
- Hand embroidery needle
- Removable fabric marker
- Play sand (available at hardware stores)
- Paper scrap
- Tape
- Spoon

Cut

Copy the Picnic Weight templates from pages 62-64.

For the cat, cut two cats from the fabric scraps. Transfer the face to one fabric cat, using a removable fabric marker. From the lining fabric, cut two weights. From the vinyl, cut one bottom.

Construct

Use ¼" seam allowances unless otherwise noted.

With wrong sides together, stitch the two weights, leaving a 2" opening.

Roll the paper scrap into a funnel shape; tape. Fill the weight opening with sand, using the funnel and a spoon. Install the machine zipper foot onto the machine, and then stitch the weight opening closed (1).

Thread a hand embroidery needle with two strands of embroidery floss. Embroider the cat face using a split stitch (2).

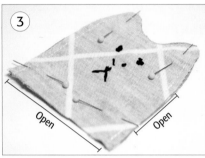

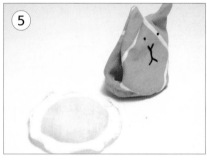

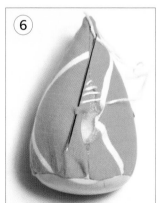

Tip: Be careful not to overfill the weight with sand.

Install the standard machine foot onto the machine. With right sides together, stitch the cat perimeter, leaving the lower edge unstitched and a 2" opening along one side edge for turning (3).

With right sides together, pin the vinyl bottom perimeter to the cat lower edge; stitch (4). Turn the cat right side out through the side opening (5). Place the weight inside the cat bottom. Firmly stuff the cat with fiberfill.

Slipstitch the opening closed (6). Pinch the cat to evenly distribute the sand and fiberfill.

Finish

Repeat to cut, embroider and construct the remaining picnic weights. When creating a chicken picnic weight, cut the beak from a small felt scrap, and then stitch it between the fabric layers according to the pattern marking. ✂

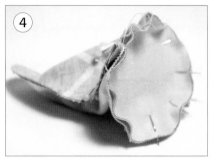

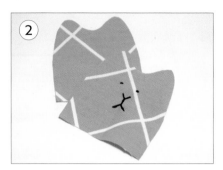

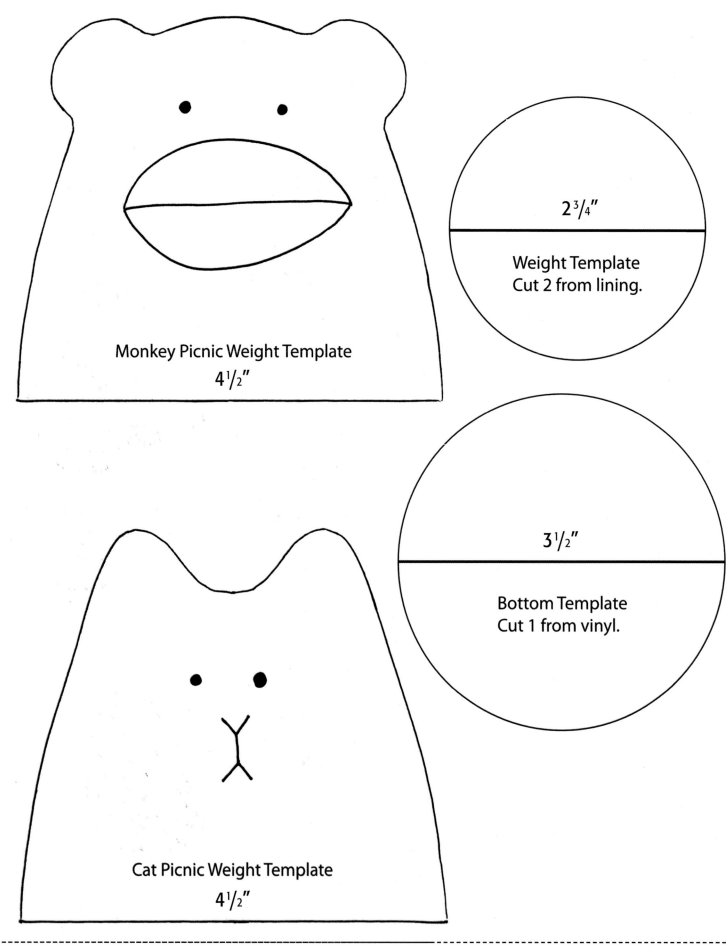

Monkey Picnic Weight Template
$4\frac{1}{2}''$

$2\frac{3}{4}''$

Weight Template
Cut 2 from lining.

$3\frac{1}{2}''$

Bottom Template
Cut 1 from vinyl.

Cat Picnic Weight Template
$4\frac{1}{2}''$

Owl Picnic Weight Template

$4\frac{1}{2}''$

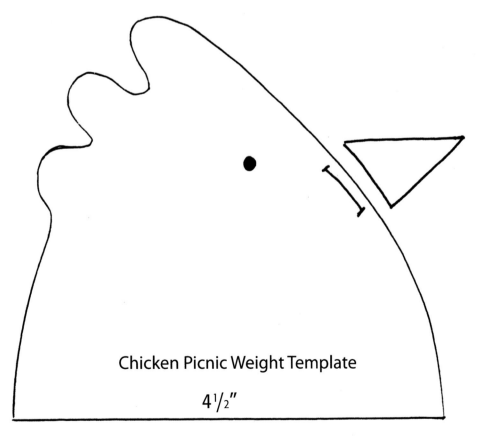

Chicken Picnic Weight Template

$4\frac{1}{2}''$

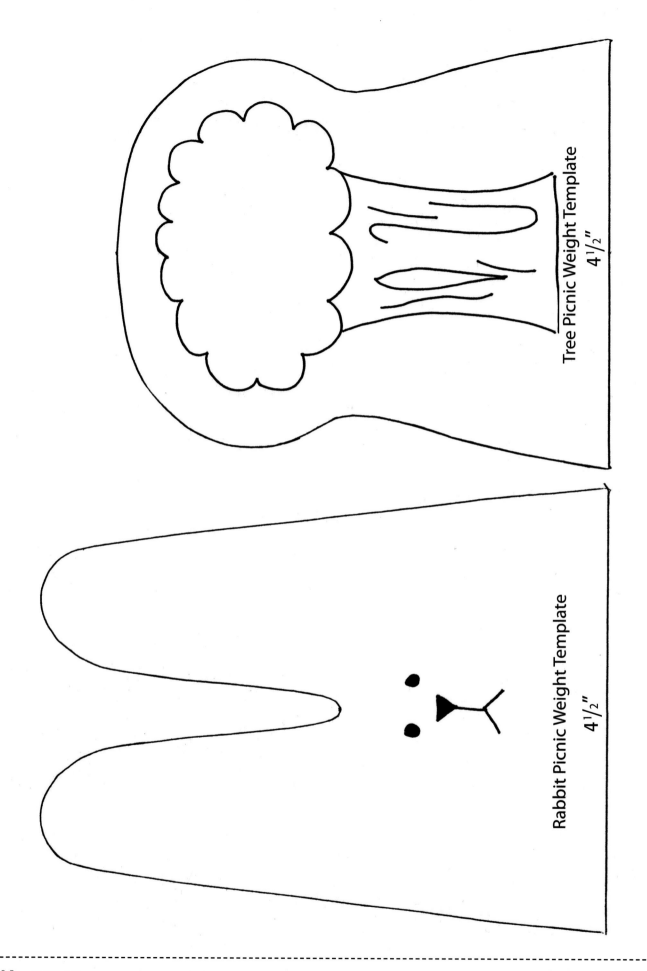

Tree Picnic Weight Template
4¹/₂″

Rabbit Picnic Weight Template
4¹/₂″